KT-480-864

just another mountain

A memoir of hope

Sarah Jane Douglas

FOREWORD BY SIR CHRIS BONINGTON

Elliott&Thompson

First published 2019 by
Elliott and Thompson Limited
2 John Street, London WC1N 2ES
www.eandtbooks.com

This paperback edition first published in 2020

ISBN: 978-1-78396-495-6

Copyright © Sarah Jane Douglas 2019

The Author has asserted her right under the Copyright, Designs and
Patents Act, 1988, to be identified as Author of this Work.

All rights reserved. No part of this publication may be reproduced, stored
in or introduced into a retrieval system, or transmitted, in any form, or by
any means (electronic, mechanical, photocopying, recording or otherwise)
without the prior written permission of the publisher. Any person who does
any unauthorised act in relation to this publication may be liable to criminal
prosecution and civil claims for damages.

9 8 7 6 5 4 3 2 1

A catalogue record for this book is available from the British Library.

Typesetting by Marie Doherty
Printed by CPI Group (UK) Ltd, Croydon, CR0 4YY

Written in loving memory of my mother and grandparents, and for my two sons, Marcus and Leon

Contents

Phase Two: Troubled Tracks

Phase Three: Steps in the Sunshine

Contents

Foreword

My own love of mountains started in the summer of 1951, at the age of sixteen, when I climbed a hill in Blackrock, a suburb of Dublin. It was certainly no mountain but it sparked a passion that led me to devote my life to climbing all over the world. I have faced the most forbidding mountains on earth and have always relished the challenge, even climbing the Old Man of Hoy, the tallest sea stack in the British Isles, to mark my eightieth birthday.

It is an experience that remains exhilarating no matter where we are in the world, or what stage of life we are in: the physical challenges of endurance; the thrill of the risks taken; the elation of reaching the summit; the joy of immersion in the rugged scenery, all of your senses in tune with the landscape you're walking through.

The mountains are also a place to seek solace. There have been many times in my life when I have found peace in such solitary and unforgiving surrounds. In times of trouble and grief, walking has seen me through.

It is for these reasons that I have so enjoyed reading of Sarah Jane Douglas's experiences, which have inspired her to find strength in the face of life's challenges. There is something universal at the heart of this book – something we can all understand, not just those of us who have grown to love the mountains. That immersing ourselves in wild landscapes can heal, motivate and inspire us is something that is beyond doubt.

Sarah's story shows that this is open to everyone; anyone can decide to go out and just start walking. To pit oneself against a summit – even a small one, in a suburb of Dublin – can be the beginning of a lifetime of adventure and discovery. I hope that this book will inspire others to do the same.

Sir Chris Bonington
2019

Prologue

Loads of people get horrible diagnoses all the time, so really it isn't anything special or extraordinary that I found myself with membership to the cancer club. To be honest I'd been expecting it, but the news still came as a swift kick to the balls. The hardest thing to get my head around was the fact that twenty years earlier I'd held my own mum's hand when breast cancer stole her life from mine. It had taken me most of my adulthood to recover from her loss.

I was twenty-four when my mum died, and it felt far too young. I wasn't ready for it – in my mind I was still a child, her child, and I needed her. But she was gone for ever. Lost without her, I spent years lurching from one distraction to the next: drinking too much, dabbling with drugs, loveless sex with too many men, motherhood. I got into trouble with the police. I wound up in a volatile marriage. Without her support, and with the subsequent deaths of my grandparents, it seemed there was no one who cared. I had my two sons, but sometimes it felt like a struggle just to keep breathing: I was at odds with the world and everything in it.

But I'd made a promise to Mum that I wouldn't give up, and the hope within, which at times seemed to have died, somehow kept flickering.

I remembered – and turned to – a world I'd once loved, a world right on my doorstep: mountains.

I'd grown up in the Scottish Highlands, so mountains had always been a big part of my life. Mum and I would often walk together, and many of my favourite memories of her are from those times. After her death, I continued to go on my own for long walks on the beach and along the river – it helped me to feel closer to her. But it was when my life started to spiral out of control that I really started to discover a passion for the outdoors. At first I started setting out for places wilder and further afield, but I soon realised I needed more of an outlet, time to escape, and eventually I sought out high tops. Proximity to nature was soothing; I felt at peace and perfectly secure in the rugged environment. The more I ventured out, the more I wanted to do and the higher I wanted to go.

I didn't know it at first, but hillwalking would be the key to turning things around. As soon as I find myself on top of a mountain I am filled with the joy of life, even more so if the summit has been hard won through tricky terrain or challenging weather. Climbing all of Scotland's highest peaks, pitting myself against nature, forced me to face up to my troubles. It reconnected me to my mum and, in getting to the marrow of my experiences, it helped me move past grief. And eventually it would help me deal with cancer. Faced with my diagnosis, there was only one thing I could do, the thing I'd come to rely on so much these last few years. I had to put one foot in front of the other and just keep walking.

FOLLOWING FOOTSTEPS

'We are no other than a moving row
Of Magic Shadow-shapes that come and go
Round with the Sun-illumined Lantern held
In Midnight by the Master of the Show'

The Rubaiyat *of Omar Khayyam,* LXVIII

CHAPTER ONE

The Hills Are Calling

Meall a' Bhuachaille
— The Shepherd's Hill, April 2008

Snowflakes floated down from a heavy alabaster sky; beyond their dot-to-dot spaces Scots pines blurred in my vision. *Delicate frozen patterns.* I tried to catch flakes on my tongue, each unique in design and without permanency. *A temporary structure, like us humans,* I thought.

I'd only been walking for ten minutes but my cheeks already felt flushed in the cold air. 'I can't believe there's so much snow!' I said out loud, looking down at my feet. They felt warm inside the brown Brashers: they had been Mum's boots but they belonged to me now. Mum had always said it wasn't good to wear other people's shoes, something about feet moulding into the insoles and the leather. If they'd been anybody else's I wouldn't be wearing them, but they were hers. I guess I wanted to be close to her in whatever way I could.

Mum had felt that walking was like a cure for duress. 'Let's get out and clear our heads,' she'd say. But equally, when life was good it had given her pleasure. Over the years we shared many walks, along cliffs and coasts, far from anyone else, but she had also liked to go out alone.

In her youth, during the 1960s, she had loved to walk barefoot whenever possible, often strolling the long, curving arm of the shingle beach near our home. Mum had been quite the hippy then, with long, dark hair that was always in a centre parting, and wearing the minimum of make-up. She made her own clothes: floaty ankle-length skirts, dresses with flower prints and blue-denim bell-bottoms teamed with vest tops. She was super-cool.

Mum hitchhiked a lot in those days too – she once went all the way from the Highlands to Roslin, near Edinburgh, 276 kilometres away. Turning up at a friend's house, she was promptly given a pair of socks and shoes. I wished I could have known her then.

Out front of my childhood home, just over the road and beyond the football pitch, was a gorse-covered raised beach – a small but steep hill known as Cromal Mount. It was Mum who first led me to its top. Each time we scaled 'Crumble Hill', as I called it, was an adventure; I would dart off ahead to find a suitable hiding place to jump out on Mum, brushing up through prickly gorse on threads of sandy trail, and both of us would arrive at the top panting from the effort. Just me and her and the world at our feet; I loved that feeling of being separated from everything below. We were up high and free like the birds in the sky.

In later years, when we'd moved to nearby Nairn, Mum and I would share walks along the town's sandy white beaches, or pass by farmers' freshly cut fields next to the river path. We would be as startled by the heron as it was by us; we'd disturbed its search for rodents and off it would fly. More often we saw the large wader standing in its one-legged pose on a rock in the river, its grey, black and white feathered body half hidden by the overhanging branches and leaves of trees. The heron was always on its own, never in a pair. And the moment it saw us – even if we were some distance away – with one beat of its slender, long wings it would take flight, so gracefully. It seemed a reclusive creature, wanting to be left alone; there had been times when Mum was like that. Out along the riverbank, grey wagtails and dippers would fly between rocks poking out of the water, and chaffinches fluttered from tree to tree. My mum loved to identify what birds she could as we went, but mostly I enjoyed our walks because they lent us quiet uninterrupted time together. I was always looking to find a way in, to be closer to her. I often wished she could talk to me in the same way I could talk to her. Sometimes it felt that while I told her everything, she was holding back. But in spite of that, to me she was more than just a mum. She was my very best friend, the person I knew I could always turn to.

Now, just as she had done, I would go out walking whatever my mood – and those moods were sinking ever lower. While I was still grieving for my mother, my marriage of two years had already started to run into difficulties, causing all the other smaller problems in life to take on horrendous proportions. As my troubles piled up, I found myself being pulled in the direction of the outdoors more and more. But it no longer seemed enough – I needed something more challenging than the low-level walking I'd been used to. I needed to take off to the mountains.

I'd always thought of hillwalking and climbing as predominantly male activities. It seemed to me that men tended to resort to strenuous physical exercise like this to work out their problems, while it was seen as more natural for women to turn to a close relative or friend for support. But I had neither. Instead, I found myself yearning to be out in the elements and wilderness. Taking refuge in solitude. Gaining perspective. So here I was in April 2008, on a steep, snowy but accessible mountain near Aviemore in the Cairngorms – running to the hills, and away from the troubles of my life.

As I contoured underneath Meall a' Bhuachaille and carried on along the valley over snow-covered boardwalks, I stopped to admire Lochan Uaine. The surface water of the small lake had frozen into iridescent, concentric rings ranging from white to deep hues of pewter where the ice was thinnest – it was like a scene from a wintry fairy tale. Thin shoots growing out thickly from the severed trunk of a tree made dark criss-cross outlines, as though the tree was finding its way back to the spring of its life.

I was an accident, born in 1972 in the Highland capital, Inverness. For the first ten years of my life home was with my mum and grandparents in the small former fishing village of Ardersier on the Moray Firth, eleven miles east of the city. We lived in a grand Edwardian red-sandstone house called Inchrye which was surrounded by mountains, and it was almost like living in a bowl: all around us we had panoramic hill views, with the great bulk of Ben Wyvis rising up above coastal cliffs on the Black Isle, the low-lying Clava Hills obscuring the great Cairngorm mountain range behind, the Great Glen headed by Meall Fuar-mhonaidh, a prominent dome-shaped hill and – the one I was most intrigued by – the wintry views across the water to the cluster of shapely Strathfarrar peaks in Ross-shire.

Grandad had been furious with Mum for falling pregnant, and if Gran had got her way I wouldn't have been born at all. But my mum kept her baby, and when I arrived into the world, kicking and screaming, my grandparents couldn't have been more supportive or loving towards her, and me. My natural father was already married to someone else, and so my mother brought me up with the help of her parents. We all lived in the family home along with my mother's teenage brother and sister, David and Penny. As both my grandad and my mum went out to work, my early memories are of Gran looking after me. She was warm and caring, and naturally I developed a strong attachment to her.

It was in 1974 that the lure of adventure stirred an inherent inquisitive impulse in me at the tender age of two. Inchrye was split over three levels, and when Gran was tied up with household chores I loved snooping around its many rooms, hiding among the fur coats in her wardrobe, sneaking up on my young aunty and getting up to unintentional mischief. But, left largely to my own devices, I would often play in the attic, where metal cases and trunks, covered in layers of dust, piqued my curiosity. Inside were all manner of curios: musty-smelling old clothes, random jigsaw pieces, Dinky cars and strange, rubbery chess moulds. Sixteen-year-old Uncle David didn't know I was there, but I heard him clattering up the spiral staircase. I spied on him as he rearranged some furniture and clambered over it. I heard the window open and watched as his body, legs and feet disappeared. I was fascinated. It wasn't long before he then reappeared through the small opening, closed the window by its long metal latch, jumped down over the furniture and clattered back down the stairs. Uncle David had been out on the roof. I didn't know what it had all been about, but he had inspired me to give it a go myself a few days later.

Poor Gran. She was outside, hanging washing on the line, when the coal-man drew up in his lorry and parked in the lane alongside the tall, pebbled garden wall. As he stood on the back of his lorry, almost ready to heave the sack of coal onto his back, he spotted me.

'There's a bairn on the roof!'

'What's that you're saying?'

'There's a bairn on the roof!' repeated the coal-man, pointing.

'Yes, it's a lovely day.'

'*No! There's a bairn on the roof!*' said the coal-man, stabbing his finger skywards in my direction.

My gran, born in Liverpool, hadn't understood either the Scottish slang or the broad accent, but she soon caught his drift when she followed his pointed digit. Dropping everything, she rushed in to get my grandad. He grabbed extending ladders from the shed, propped them against the wall of the kitchen extension, climbed onto its roof and then onto the pitched roof of the building. Sitting on warm slates in the winter sunshine I was quite content, captivated by the distant snow-topped mountains beyond the waters of the inner Moray Firth. Quiet as a mouse and unperturbed – but definitely stuck – I waited to be carried down, pinned against my grandad's chest by the firm clutch of his strong arm. And all I could think was how much I wanted to go to those snowy mountains.

I was certainly finding out all about snowy mountains now. Blizzards and whiteout conditions engulfed me as I shouldered my way towards the top of Meall a' Bhuachaille. All the footprints I'd been following were quickly obliterated by fresh snow, but I wasn't concerned; there was only one way to go and that was up. *Holy fuck it's wild, but it's great!* I thought, as I grinned and gave out a howl – there wasn't a soul in sight, and even if there had been it was impossible to be heard over the bellowing wind.

As I reached the cairn on the 810m peak I yelled out again as I spun about in celebration: my first hillwalk, all on my own.

I took off my rucksack to get a drink but the zip had frozen and my efforts to yank it open were in vain. Now I was also feeling cold. Snow whirled in frenzy around me. I looked at my surroundings, hastily trying to gather my bearings while realising that it had only taken that brief moment of spinning to become disorientated. I was at the top, so I simply had to go down, but which way?

I turned my back to the buffeting wind. There was nothing to see. I was enveloped by an impenetrable wall of white. I cursed myself for not having a map or compass, but then what good would either be when I didn't really know how to use them? I cursed myself again. Fanny.

I had climbed Meall a' Bhuachaille once before; I'd done it the previous summer with my stepdad Frank and was sure I remembered the route – however, my present situation seemed anything but simple. As my mind reached into the past, desperately trying to clutch at any tiny fragment of conversation we might have had about the way off this mountain, I thought of Frank with his new family: he would be with them, safe, warm and tucked up indoors, but by fuck I wished he was here instead.

I think I have to go straight over this summit, down the other side, and just make sure I keep left. I vaguely remembered wide, open moorland that lay to the right of the hill and didn't want to end up wandering around lost down there either. Turning back round, I went to pick up my bag, which I'd left by the cairn, and promptly sank deep into the snow. My foot had stepped into nothing, and for a split-second I thought I was falling through a crevasse and was going to die. Waist deep, I hit solid ground. I freed myself by sprawling across the snow, rolling, sliding and then scrambling, laughing with embarrassment at my own stupidity. Somewhere in the clouds a helicopter flew close by. 'Maybe it's for me,' I joked. 'Right, come on, blockhead. Let's get below the treeline and you'll be fine then.'

My favoured method of descent was by sliding on my back-side, and I was glad to have decent waterproofs. But overall, I was not best prepared; my inexperience of mountains and lack of any sense of fear were childlike. The real risks of winter walking hadn't entered into my head.

When there were no clear spaces to slide, I walked. The aro-matic scent of pines filled my lungs and memory on that crisp afternoon, and aside from being stabbed by twigs and needles from low branches as I brushed a way downwards, I felt true con-tentment: I didn't have to think about trying to feel happy, I just was. Busy with the task at hand, there was no room in my mind to dwell on the sorrows or anxieties that otherwise overshadowed my life. I was free, living in the moment. Maybe that had been the lure of long walks for my mum.

From a high stance on the steep, wooded hillside I saw what I thought was a track a couple of hundred metres below – there was a bright-yellow shape on it that looked human. I felt like a lost adventurer who had just discovered a way out of the most hazardous and wild environment known to man, and I wanted to catch up with that person – or people.

It took longer than anticipated, but after a last hurdle – squelching through some sticky black bog – I reached the path. The bright yellow was a jacket worn by one of a trio, all of whom were studiously looking at what I thought was a map, but when I was almost upon them I realised it was a GPS. I didn't know anything much about GPS units then, but it didn't matter. All I cared about was finding out where I was – and the thought of getting back to my car was hugely appealing. My feet were ready to be released from Mum's Brashers, my toes felt fiery and desperate to be relieved from their boot-prison and rubbed.

I moved forward to say hello to the small group. With brief greetings over, it transpired that my saviours were as happy to have met me because they were hoping that *I* could help *them*. They didn't have a clue how to work the GPS. So we all walked back and forth and around and around together. I was beginning to wonder if we'd ever find our way back when, for the second time, I heard the unmistakable sound of air slapping off rotor blades. A yellow Sea King hovered overhead, preparing to land in a nearby field. I dashed up a small, steep bank to see it and was surprised by the unexpected sight of the sprawling outdoor-activity centre, Glenmore Lodge. I squealed with delight; my car was parked just beyond the building.

Boots and waterproofs off, I was on the road – wanting and not wanting to go home. The day hadn't gone entirely to plan; weather conditions in combination with my lack of experience and equipment could have spelt disaster. I had, however, enjoyed myself to the full, battling the elements but 'living to tell the tale' of my first autonomous venture into the hills. It had been invigorating, and I had felt alive in a way that I had not done for so many years.

Eleven years actually, ever since Mum died.

Back at home, I thought of her as I placed her boots by the hearth to dry. The brown Brashers had looked after me and kept my feet warm at the start of the day, but now they felt heavy and smelt of leathery dampness. I would definitely need my own pair at some point. Still, those sodden boots had connected me to her out on the hillside, had helped me feel closer to her. How I wished right then that I could tell her about the day I'd spent. She'd have shaken her head disapprovingly but would have said she was glad I'd had a good time and that I'd probably learnt a valuable lesson. When she said these sorts of things I usually hadn't learnt much at all and would go on to make similar mistakes but in a different way. Mum had always erred on the side of caution, preparing well for most things, preferring to reduce the element of risk. We both had to learn that sometimes life has other plans.

CHAPTER TWO

Coincidence or Fate

Back to Bhuachaille, May 2008/
Bynack More — The Big Cap, May 2008

Driving back from Meall a' Bhuachaille that day, as the miles between me and home decreased the familiar feeling of dread crept in. On the hill it had been just me pitted against nature and the rugged terrain. But now I had to return to my real life: back to supply teaching, while waiting to begin my probation year; back to horrible neighbours and a leaking roof; back to the troubles of my marriage. I was already yearning to feel that sense of escape again, and so not long after my snowy adventure I returned to Meall a' Bhuachaille with my husband, Sam. I hoped he would feel a connection to nature, as I had, and share that sense of life's worries being put firmly into perspective. I hoped it would become something we could do together, a new common ground, reaching for boots instead of a bottle.

I'd met Sam in 2004. It was seven years after Mum's death and now, with two small boys at my heels, I was working weekend shifts at a pub, and I hadn't been there long before the pub's leasehold was taken over by Sam. At forty-five he was older than me by thirteen years, but he didn't look it. I liked to watch him as he stood at the jukebox. He was tall, had a strong jawline, jet-black hair and cool sideburns. Always smartly dressed in suits and with a broad Glaswegian accent, he had the look and sound of a gangster; he had edge – I liked that. And he was what my grandad would have called a man's man, old school when it came to paying for dinner or walking on the outside of the pavement. At first he made me feel like I was the centre of his world.

We became more deeply involved when his marriage failed, and when my ninety-one-year-old grandfather's health was declining quickly. Neither of us was in a good place emotionally, but, as fools do, and ignoring the sage advice my grandad had offered back in my student days, I rushed headlong into the new romance.

Sam had a huge capacity for kindness and was great fun, but when he was fuelled by alcohol he was wild – we both were. I was fascinated by his darker side. I wanted to unearth its roots and understand him . . . or maybe I thought he was just like me, lost and lonely . . . maybe I thought we could save each other.

Drink was always involved when we first started seeing each other, and I was too busy being caught up in the excitement of our flirtations to think too much about how wrecked either of us would get. At the end of our evenings, when I would leave Sam and go home, he came across all hurt and dejected – as if he couldn't bear us to be parted. Nobody had ever looked at me in such a way before.

After I gradually introduced him to my sons, Marcus and Leon, Sam moved in with me. For a while I felt he gave me stability. He treated my erratic moods with kindness and a hug, and took care of me when I was low. And he was understanding when dementia tightened its grip on my grandfather, and I wanted to spend more time with him and give some extra help.

During his army career my grandfather had been well respected, with a reputation of being firm but fair; and it's true to say this was the case at home too. He'd once been a good footballer and won loads of medals; he was an even better tennis player, but more surprisingly he was an excellent Highland dancer. He had never been one to boast and he'd never been one to take his work home with him. But now, both in body and mind, dementia had reduced him to a shadow of his former self.

I remember first noticing the signs when I saw him greeted warmly by an old colleague who seemed to know him very well, and who spoke with him for several minutes.

'Who was that?' I asked, after the man walked away.

'I haven't a bloody clue, dear,' came the answer.

Sam never knew the man my grandad had once been, but I was glad they had met. Sam even asked him for my hand in marriage. Poor Grandad, he was confused. He mistakenly thought that Sam was an officer and asked what regiment he was attached to before shaking his hand warmly and saying, 'I'd be honoured to have you marry my daughter.' I doubt my grandad would have been so approving if he'd known the troubles and arguments that went on between us, even then.

When we drank, Sam was always first to tip over the edge. If I had been my younger self I would have carried on drinking too, descending with him into a well of depression and self-pity. I understood it was the drink talking when Sam's insecurities roared to the surface, but my best efforts to placate and reassure him were wasted.

As time went on, I kept making excuses to myself and often recited internal lists as to why we should stay together. At the top was always the hope that he would change. Things hadn't worked out with either of my children's fathers and I didn't want to fail at another relationship. My kids liked him and Sam was fond of them too. I was sure that having a constant father figure in their lives could only be a positive thing for them, and their happiness was paramount. In short, I convinced myself that I needed him. And, of course, anything was better than being alone, so I clung on. Despite the upsets and fights, I'd attempted so many times to reconcile the feelings I had about my marriage: and now the hills were a last resort for its rescue.

To avoid repeating my previous walk exactly, my plan was to do the Meall a' Bhuachaille circuit in reverse, hiking over the smaller tops Craigowrie and Creagan Gorm first. It would make for a longer and more satisfying day out, and there would be less chance of meeting anybody else on this route. It would be just us and the elements, exactly how I liked it. But this time I made sure I checked the weather forecast – and that I had a map and compass, even though I wasn't a hundred per cent sure I knew what I was doing with either. Of course there was also the not so small matter of childcare to sort out. Finding someone to look after the boys wasn't always the easiest thing to arrange. Without having my own mum to turn to, I asked my children's paternal grandparents for help. Though they had contact with their grandchildren there was no real relationship between me and them, so I'd felt awkward for asking, as though I was taking advantage when I knew I'd be gone for the best part of a whole day. What sweet relief it was when they'd said yes to my request.

Although the hills we were going to do weren't especially high by comparison with nearby Cairngorm, they could still hold on to a good covering of snow even well into May. And since I'd only been here a week earlier, I fully expected to find the peaks still under their wintry blanket. I suggested repeatedly that Sam change his clothing, but he insisted jeans would be fine.

'Sam,' I said, 'I don't know much about hillwalking, but I do know that jeans are a terrible choice in wet weather.'

'How's that then?' he asked.

'They hold water.'

'Yeah, but snow's different, it's drier than rain.'

We hadn't even reached the top of the first hill before Sam's clothes were saturated. Not only had he become sodden by trudging through almost knee-deep crunchy snow, but he also fell into a muddy and watery hole. At work two nights earlier he had accidentally chopped off the end of his index finger in the safe door when it had swung shut. Preserving the tip of his finger in ice, he took it to hospital to have it stitched back on. And so the vision of his white, massively bandaged finger pointing skywards in *Saturday Night Fever* fashion was hilarious as he struggled to free himself. Weak with laughter, I helped extract him from the muddy breach but, man, was he annoyed.

Leaving Sam and his bad mood trailing behind, I arrived at the first peak on the ridge and perched myself on a rock. Surprised to discover that Sam and I weren't the only ones who had thought to come this way, I introduced myself to two men who were sitting against the summit cairn.

'I was here last week,' I said. 'I climbed up Meall a' Bhuachaille in a whiteout and got totally disorientated. I'm glad the weather's better today!'

'You wouldn't happen to know Dawn Main by any chance?' asked the older of the two men.

'Yes! I would!' I said. 'I know her from school. How do you know her?'

'She's a colleague of ours. So you'll be the mad pal she was telling us about who got lost in the snow,' teased the other guy, Ollie, whose baggy trousers and black jacket disguised a tall, heavy-set frame.

We were laughing and marvelling at the coincidence when Sam reached us; I could tell by his face that all he wanted to do was turn round and go back to the car, so I quickly introduced him to the two men and explained the connection. Sam appeared more at ease on the hill with the distraction of male company and so the four of us ended up carrying along the ridge together, but before a final climb up to the top of Meall a' Bhuachaille Sam called it a day.

'Sarah! If you need a hill buddy, get Dawn to let me know. I'd be happy to join you,' Ollie called back. I smiled and waved as we travelled in our different directions. Neither of us could know it then but, after that chance encounter, Ollie's part in my hillwalking career would turn out to be significant.

Sam and I navigated our way back down, along tracks and fire breaks through Queen's Forest to the road and then finally back to our parked car, much to Sam's relief.

'Did you enjoy our day?' I asked him, as we drank a post-hill dram at home.

'Hmm. I couldn't be arsed doing that every weekend. Too boring just walking up a hill and then back down again,' he answered.

Ten minutes later he was flaked out on the sofa. I looked at his peaceful face and was disappointed that he hadn't felt the same sense of wonderment and freedom that I felt on the mountains. But my plan had partly worked, because at least he wasn't getting drunk – there would be no shit tonight.

To get ideas for walks I bought a popular book on Scotland's highest mountains. Inside its covers were route descriptions, grid references for start points and estimated times for how long each walk should take. A world of possibilities for new adventures – for escaping my troubles – literally opened up for me with the turn of each page. There were coloured drawings showing relief, rivers, summits, and a broken red line with little arrowheads even indicated direction of travel. Perfect for a birdbrain like me. As I'd flipped through the book I came across what I decided would be the next walk, Bynack More in the Cairngorm range. The route looked easy enough, and its start point at Glenmore Lodge and the first section up this mountain were now familiar to me.

It was the week after our first outing together and a scorcher of a day. The sky was a brilliant blue with just a few scattered white clouds. The journey across Dava Moor towards the Cairngorms was quiet; Sam had taken some convincing to come out again so soon.

He was silent as we set out walking, no doubt brooding about having to spend a whole day in the outdoors, but I still hoped there was a chance he'd fall in love with the mountains. 'Come and see Lochain Uaine,' I enthused. 'It's like an amazing little secret tucked away from the masses, so perfectly unspoilt.' Eventually he agreed, but he seemed to be regretting it already.

We took a brief detour from our path to Ryvoan bothy, at the head of the pass. Once an important drovers' road, it linked other tracks stretching off to the north, or heading east to the coast. Its interior was dingy, with only a dull light cast through the small, cobwebbed window, but its sturdy stone walls conveyed a sense of history. I imagined times when shepherds would have taken grateful shelter here. However, in the mild weather it smelt like wet dog.

Sam was unimpressed. I was going to have my work cut out trying to entertain him. I wished I hadn't been so insistent that he join me. I felt resentful that the effort involved in trying to please him was going to spoil my own sense of enjoyment. This wasn't how it was meant to be.

Returning to a junction in the track, we branched off in an easterly direction. Before crossing a wooden bridge over the River Nethy we came to a long section of trail comprising loose stones, varying in size and stability. Sam complained that the rough terrain was causing pain to flare up in his knee, but he soldiered on.

It seemed a long walk in the heat as we followed the footpath south-east over the lower shoulder of Bynack More. I decided to distract Sam by walking ahead with my butt exposed. It had the desired effect. He roared with laughter at the sight of my wobbling white posterior which, with a rapid yank of my trousers, was quickly concealed just before the first people we encountered saw more than they had bargained for. The old boy looked like an ageing Crocodile Dundee in his Australian cork hat, beating the trail ahead of his wife.

'You're the first people we've seen in five days,' she said. 'We've been wild-camping. We've come from Loch Avon and I'm so looking forward to reaching Glenmore Lodge and civilisation!'

'I hope I'm doing stuff like that when I'm their age,' I said to Sam, once they were gone and out of earshot.

'Rock on, Granny,' he laughed, and I did too. But deep down inside, while I did have hopes that I would be adventuring into my twilight years, I didn't think I'd be doing so with Sam.

As we continued to ascend Bynack More the winds picked up, blowing across austere and barren windswept plains of muted browns and purples. Taking shelter, we stopped to have lunch behind a huge hunk of granite, where a friendly dog appeared and tried to join us for a piece of quiche. '*Fuck off!*' I said through my teeth while directing my smile towards its approaching owners.

Sam petted the animal. 'Aww. She's only cranky 'cause she's hungry. She disnae want your big doggy slavers dripping ower her lunch when you were probably licking your baws ten minutes ago.' He could be affectionate and funny, and I wished that was how things were between us all the time. Mum had said you only got to really know a person by living with them for a couple of years. After our four years together, I could now say I really knew Sam.

When we reached the 1,090m summit of Bynack More the wind had strengthened; snot now streamed from my nostrils like horizontally blown, translucent windsocks. I loved the ferocity and felt an affiliation with the wildness: it was like a physical manifestation of what raged through my being.

Scrambling up over the higgledy-piggledy maze of giant granite tors, I soaked in my surroundings. From here, the north-eastern fringe of the Cairngorms, there was nothing to interrupt the views over Moray. Meall a' Bhuachaille and its pine-covered lower slopes, which teemed with all kinds of insect and bird life, seemed left far behind. It was a different world up here of rough weathered bedrock: the height and exposure gave it an Arctic climate. It was truly wild and empty, and I could imagine how inhospitable a place winter would make it. As I turned round, the mountain seemed much smaller, dominated suddenly by the massive shoulders of Cairn Gorm, its magnificent corries and big, rounded plateaux beyond. The wind caused a milky haze to lightly veil the views, and Sam created his own fog by puffing on a cigarette as he lay slumped against one of the tors.

Neither marred my enjoyment. But I didn't experience that same sense of freedom I'd felt walking on my own or with my mother: I hadn't been able to fully lose myself in the day because I'd been preoccupied with how to keep Sam happy – as I so often was, I realised. I had married him because I was looking for the security I no longer had from having my own family. But being out on the mountains with him, unable to share the exhilaration and joy of the experience, was helping me gain some clarity on my relationship. My attempt at finding some common ground for us to connect, to save our marriage, was failing. I was going to have to accept that my new-found passion wasn't ever going to appeal to him. For me our walk on Bynack More marked both the beginning of an enduring love for the mountains and a long and drawn-out end to my marriage to Sam.

We returned to Glenmore by retracing our steps – painful ones for Sam when his footwear came apart. At first the sole of his boot flapped open, just at the toes, but it wasn't long before the whole lot gave up and gave way.

'That's the last hill am ever climbin', Sayree. Never again.'

In truth, our relationship had been destined for failure from the beginning.

With hindsight, I knew the warning signs had been there all along. But at the time I didn't recognise them and so, a year and a half after my grandfather died, in 2006, Sam and I married. I'd wanted our wedding to take place in the chapel at Fort George where my grandfather, a major in the Queen's Own Cameron Highlanders, had been quartermaster during the 1960s.

The Fort was at the furthest point north-west of the village, within sight of my childhood home. It had been built in the eighteenth century, after the Jacobite rising of 1745, on a level spit of land jutting out into the Moray Firth, guarding it at its narrowest point. It is an impressive place. The ramparts, more than a kilometre in length, enclose an area the size of five football pitches. Pristine green grassy slopes lead up to projecting bastions and redoubts. Every wall is covered with guns and big black cannons remain fixed in place, pointing out across the water. The barracks are still used by the military, but much of the rest of the site is run by Historic Scotland and is open to the public.

I loved the Fort. It was steeped in family history. In the museum my grandad's medals and regimental claymore are part of the exhibit. I'd been christened there; my name is framed in the Cradle Roll on the chapel wall. Mum had once worked behind its great sandstone walls too, at first in the dental clinic and then as verger of the church (not a virgin of the church as I'd mistakenly told people). It was where Mum had been meant to get married to her first love – and was where she did eventually marry Frank.

I had warm memories of trips to the Fort as well. When I was small Mum would load me onto the back of her bike and off we'd go, her legs doing all the pedalling while I enjoyed the wind in my hair, my little fingers sticky with a melting mini-milk lolly. There were other days when, unnoticed by Gran, I'd steal out of the back garden and range along the squidgy, waterlogged sands of the beach with the intention of visiting Mum at her work. She and I had walked this way a million times when the tide was out, around the base of the Fort's sloping perimeter walls, me searching for jellyfish and squashing flat the wiggly worm casts while she sang a song to herself.

It had been an important place for me and for Mum, and I had my heart set on getting married there. Because of my grandfather's old role as quartermaster, special permission was granted and my wedding ceremony went ahead. We had our wedding photographs taken on the battlements, where as a child I'd run around wild, loose and carefree. But with each picture Sam was becoming more impatient. He wanted to get to the party.

The reception was held at the Gun Lodge Hotel, back in the village. Also built in the eighteenth century, it had been home and stables for the high-ranking officers at the Fort. It became a hospital for a short while, but after falling into disrepair during the 1960s it was bought up and reopened as a hotel. Mum had worked there too, behind the bar; she'd fetch me home salt and vinegar crisps and a lemonade, and tell me snippets of silly things that some of the customers said or did. Sometimes men who had a fancy for her would give her presents to give to me; once some guy bought a whole tray of plastic gold and silver rings with coloured gems, setting my little-girl eyeballs spiralling in their sockets. But, most of all, I loved hearing Mum's story about Georgina the ghost who haunted the pub, and I would make her repeat that same tale over and over again. I remembered all these things as I cut the wedding cake with Sam. We danced, we sang, and we drank till it was time to leave.

Inchrye, our old family home, was only a stone's throw away from the pub. The house had changed hands several times since my grandad had sold it back in 1984, and now it was being run as a B&B. This was where Sam and I would spend our first night as a married couple. 'You're staying at Inchrye? That's a bit macabre, isn't it?' Mum's older brother Jimmy said as we tripped out into the chilly car park. His words wounded me. These places – the Fort, the Gun Lodge, the house – connected me to my mother and grandparents. Why was it wrong to want to keep those fond memories alive?

The owners of Inchrye, learning that I had grown up there, gave us a tour of the house the following day. I disguised my broken heart through smiles and nods of approval at the structural changes. Every room had been altered; the old bedroom I'd shared with Mum, where she'd play her Leonard Cohen and Donovan records, was unrecognisable. It wasn't the home I remembered. My hand glided down the banister and memories filled my head as I walked down the last flight of stairs: I could see my grandad, there at the foot of the staircase, and smell the paraffin from the heater he'd just lit to take the chill off the cold midwinter air. And then a memory of Gran, smiling at me as she opened the door of the dining room to show me the incredible feast of jellies, cakes and sandwiches she had prepared for my birthday tea, then saying, 'Well, there it is. You can like it or lump it.' I smelt cigarette smoke intermingled with the aroma of whisky, and heard the rapid chattering and laughter of my grandparents as they entertained guests in 'the posh front room', my mother asking what I was doing up so late but letting me sit up and join in the fun for a while.

I'd spent countless happy hours playing in the garden on the swing my grandad built, and roaming around after him as he pushed the lawnmower and hoed the soil. I'd pester him for fruit off the trees and he'd always choose me the juiciest plum. But when Sam and I were led outside I found it hard not to cry. The beautiful borders, host to the glorious colours of summer flowers and plants, the lawns, greenhouse, fruit and vegetable patches – everything was gone, replaced by an acre of chipped stones, two wooden sheds, a caravan and an old red telephone box. Every fibre of my body groaned. I wanted everything to go back to how it used to be and, as I ached for my family, I thought my uncle had been right in a way: it had been a mistake to stay at the old house. Deep down, even then, I think I knew it had also been a mistake to get married.

CHAPTER THREE

Doomed Champagne and Mountain Magic

Beinn Eighe – The File Hill, June 2008

'How do you know where you're going when you're in a car?' asked Frank.

'I read road signs,' I replied.

'Yes, but when you get in your car, how do you know how to get there?'

'Because I never go anywhere that I don't know how to get to . . . Ohhhh, do you mean have I a road map?'

'Yes.'

'Nah, I don't have a road map.'

Frank drove for a further ten minutes. 'Well,' he said, breaking the silence, 'here's the thing now . . . we've taken the wrong road.'

I groaned inwardly. An extra 35 miles had been added to the journey to Torridon and the mystery mountain where Frank was taking us – me, his new wife Irina and her eleven-year-old son Roman. After that last disastrous walk with Sam I had wanted to get out again but didn't have anyone else I could think of to ask. Then I'd remembered Frank. It had been quite some time since we'd last had contact, but when I asked him if he would come hillwalking he was enthusiastic and said he had a place in mind where we could go. I was happy to leave the details to him – checking the weather, the route, what time we should set off – but I hadn't thought that he'd bring his new family along too; I was a bit disappointed. Not because I disliked them, but because conversation was virtually impossible. Irina's English was only marginally better than my Russian. Besides, I had been hoping it would just be Frank and me because I'd wanted to talk about, and remember, Mum.

Frank was the living connection to my mum. After she had died, we'd clung to each other for a while, bound together because we both loved her. Although in some ways he still felt like an anchor to my past, eventually, like two separate threads coiled around the same reel, we had started to unravel from one another and the distance had seemed to grow between us with each passing year.

Five months earlier, at the start of January, Frank had remarried. He'd had other love interests since Mum had died, but his getting hitched made everything different. It wasn't as though I had expected or wanted him to remain faithful to my mother's memory, but the child in me resented him for being happy and for moving on.

It was almost midday by the time we arrived at our destination. 'One of us needs to drive the car about another mile further on, to where we'll finish the walk,' Frank said, looking in my direction.

'I suppose that'll be me then,' I replied with resignation, but secretly glad that I wouldn't have to try to communicate with Irina and Roman.

'Good girl,' he laughed, then added, 'there should be a small parking area on your right-hand side, you won't miss it. We'll wait here.'

It took me half an hour to ditch the car and make it back to them, and then finally we were on our way. But within twenty minutes of walking we were already stopping for our first rest. Irina was tired, and I was thinking, *You've got to be kidding* – we had just passed a copse of trees and were still on the flat!

The trail we were on was easy to follow as it wound gently upwards, steepening as it climbed towards a grassy-floored corrie, a glacially scooped-out hollow in the side of the mountain, and since the route was obvious and the weather dry and fine, I carried on ahead of the others even though I didn't have a map – if I was unsure of where I should be going I knew I could wait for them. Frank was in charge, which made me feel safe, and so, like the giddiness you feel after guzzling a glass of fizz, I was able to freely enjoy the exhilaration of simply being on the mountain. Although I would have preferred his company on this occasion, I enjoyed the solitude. I could hear only the panting of my own breath and each step of my boots as they connected to the ground. The sun was shining and there were no elements to battle. I was able to lose myself in thought instead of concerning myself with – as Frank called them – 'route logistics'.

Pausing briefly, I looked behind: my three walking companions were dots almost consumed by the vastness of wild country, and they didn't seem to be making much progress. I carried on. Ascending the steep corrie headwall was a formidable task – I felt like a spider, using both my feet and hands to grip and clutch at grassy tufts till I made it to the top, where I was confronted by a staggering and intimidating view. Catching my breath, I stood transfixed. My eyes met with the scariest-looking mountain I'd ever seen – a vision of breathtaking beauty, horror and impossible enormity all rolled into one. It was Liathach: a towering fortress with terraced cliffs of sandstone topped with quartzite, otherworldly in appearance and so utterly extraordinary I couldn't quite take in what I was looking at. It was both real and not real. *People have climbed that?* Of course I knew people had, I just couldn't comprehend how when it looked so completely impregnable (yet I too would eventually scale its heights). I stared at that mountain opposite for twenty minutes before Frank appeared over the crest of the headwall.

'At last!' I exclaimed. He just laughed.

Mum and Frank had often gone off on short hillwalks or coastal routes, and on occasion I'd go with them. We got used to walking together efficiently; I hadn't expected to have to wait around for the others to catch up today.

'It was never like this when we were walking with Mum; at least we all kept the same pace,' I said. 'Remember that walk we did at Kilmuir on the Black Isle?'

'Oh yes,' he said with delight. 'Right . . . don't panic, but run! Those cows were seriously chasing us through that field. Didn't we have to jump over a fence or something?' Frank said, now laughing hard. The three of us had enjoyed some lovely walks there; goats roamed the coastal cliffs, gulps of cormorants clustered on volcanic rock and huge birds of prey hovered above.

'Wasn't that the same day you stuck a dead bird on a stick and chased Mum and me?'

'Mmmmm, baby,' Frank said in one of his funny voices. 'Mum was cross about that. She liked her birds. She was very upset when we saw that gull trapped on a rock, surrounded by the sea. Didn't it have a broken wing or something?'

'That's right, I'd forgotten about that. She was upset because she couldn't do anything to help it.'

'Yes, Mum was a very special lady,' he said with affection.

Irina and Roman continued to make their way up, but now I didn't mind the extra wait. I was enjoying listening to Frank, who had entered full-blown storytelling mode.

'My best walk with Mum was one we did at Torr Achilty, it was a *verrry* hot day,' he said, rolling his 'r's, 'and we drove about half a mile to a quiet area on the River Conon. The river was well hidden from sight by lots of foliage. Mum and I went for a naked swim.' After pausing he added, 'It was quite brave of her.' Although I didn't really want to know about Mum stripping off, I did like Frank sharing that story. There was so much I didn't get to know about her.

Keen to get moving again, I asked, 'Which way from here?'

Frank pointed me towards a scree slope on the right. 'I've got a surprise for you, but I'll tell you at the end of phase three of the walk,' he said. There was no point quizzing him about the surprise – he loved his little games – so I playfully rolled my eyes and shook my head. On I went alone, wondering what on earth the surprise was, while he dutifully waited for Irina and Roman.

We got on now, but I hadn't always liked Frank. I'd behaved awkwardly when, in my early teens, he'd got together with Mum; actually, I was the original demon-spawned child from hell. Back then I'd seen him as a threat and would constantly try to find faults in him. What an asshole I'd been, and Frank had taken it.

I think I'd struggled to accept him for the same reason I'd struggled to accept any of my mum's boyfriends. I couldn't bear thinking of them as a potential father because none of them came close to being the man who should have filled that role. A man who had shaped my mum's life, and mine, and whose presence I felt throughout my childhood and beyond. Poor Frank had had some big shoes to fill.

During the spring of 1973 Mum had got the job as verger in the chapel at the Fort. At this time, among other army units, the Fort contained the Joint Services Mountain Training Centre, to which arrived a young new Chief Instructor, Major Gerry Owens. A bachelor and keen sportsman in his early thirties, he already had a formidable reputation as a Himalayan mountaineer. When he and my mum met, the pair fell deeply in love.

Without reservation Gerry was well liked by all the family. Gran thought he was dashing; his handsome, angular face was framed by sandy curls, his athletic build was clad in stylish garb, and he was charming. Grandad approved of him too.

Those who knew him best would say that Gerry was a good companion with a huge capacity for fun, often making digs but always in friendship. On the mountains his determination and resolve were unstoppable. On one occasion he was on an army mountaineering expedition in northern India, climbing up a vertical rock face, when the loose snow all the way up the ridge gave way. Luckily, he and his climbing partner were firmly attached to the rocks as the avalanche thundered down around them. According to his partner, Gerry was silent and calm during the entire ordeal, and when it was over simply finished the route without a word in response to his partner's exclamations of relief. He was as hard as nails and gave himself – and others – no quarter. But with my mother and me he was tender and caring. Because of his love of being out in the wild, amid nature, Gerry encouraged my mum to join him on days out.

Walking hadn't really been Mum's thing back in those days. Her older brother, my uncle Jimmy, had told me he'd been surprised when she got together with Gerry as she'd never struck him as an outdoors sort of person. During the summer of 1973, when he had arrived home on a rare visit from university, he spotted two familiar figures making their way to the house. He remembered being amused at the spectacle of his sister, looking distinctly unimpressed, with her dark hair stuck to the sides of her rain-soaked face and clothes sagging under the weight of the water. Gerry strode up the rose-bordered path with a huge grin on his face and called out to my mother, lagging a good fifty yards behind, 'Hurry up! Come and greet your brother!' Gerry enthusiastically described what a great time they had had. Uncle Jimmy said Mum looked as though she had never spent a worse day in her life, but gave a bright smile and agreed that it had been 'great'. My uncle thought the relationship wouldn't last, but he was proved wrong as my mum developed an enduring love of the outdoors life, and for Gerry.

Gerry was away a lot for his job with the army, but he would always send my mum a postcard or a tourist guidebook with a scribbled message to let her know he was thinking about her. Two years after they met, he was to be posted to Norway. He asked Mum to go with him; she accepted. But when she announced the plans to Gran and Grandad they put their foot down. I had been born out of wedlock, and despite their approval of Gerry they would not allow Mum to live with him outside of marriage. This caused a big problem between the pair, and for a few weeks they were apart; but finally, on Christmas Day 1974, Gerry took the plunge and asked Mum to be his wife. Everybody was delighted. Predictably unconventional, Mum said she didn't want an engagement ring, so instead Gerry presented her with a hinged gold bangle engraved with a fine leaf pattern: she loved it and it rarely left her wrist.

With his posting to Norway coming up at the end of summer, Mum and Gerry planned a short engagement. Their vows were to be taken in the chapel at the Fort in June, a few weeks after he was due to return from a Himalayan expedition to Nuptse with the Army Mountaineering Association. It was a training exercise for the army's plans to summit Everest the following year and, as one of their strongest climbers, Gerry was a forerunner for the team. He left in mid February and Mum wrote to him at least once a week while they were apart.

And then, six weeks before the ceremony, it all came to a catastrophic end.

Though I was only a little child of about two and a half years old, the scene and exchanges are clear in my mind: some things just stick. I was sensitive to my mother's moods and I had noticed a change. Despite the sunshine of late spring an oppressive darkness made its presence felt, and the silence that had fallen on Inchrye was disquieting. Something was very wrong, I sensed it.

The morning was bright. The sun reflected off the two-tone small pink squares on the lino of our bedroom floor, the hearth lay empty and the radio sat in obedient silence above it on the mantelpiece. My mum and I stood between the bed and the chest of drawers near the door. I was small and she was so tall.

'When's Gerry coming back?' I asked, looking up to her face. She turned away from me.

'He's not.' Her tone was cold and unemotional. She walked away, leaving me in the room on my own.

In those early days we shared a bed. I'd wake up in the night and rest my little leg over the top of hers, but now she would push it off and turn her back to me. I suppose this was really the first time I felt a sense of being shut out. It wasn't that she didn't love me. She did. But what I didn't yet know was that she had become consumed with grief: Gerry was dead.

I had known nothing about my biological father when I was growing up, so later, when anybody asked about my dad, I told them he was dead. The person I was referring to was Gerry, even though I hadn't really known anything much about him either. But those people who had asked the question would offer expressions of condolence followed invariably by the question: 'What happened?'

'He was a mountaineer and he died in a fall,' I would say – that much was true. That was what I had told my teacher when both Mum and I started at the same school, her as a teacher and me as a pupil, and I had cringed afterwards thinking, *Ah no, what if Mrs Miller questions Mum in the staffroom?* I hadn't wanted to cause upset. But if it ever was mentioned, Mum never let on.

Gerry's early death had robbed my mother of a husband and me of a father. Maybe it wouldn't have worked out for them, and he might have turned out not to be a brilliant stepdad, but it was something neither of us had the chance to find out. I'd been told by both my aunt and my grandparents that after Gerry learnt of my roof escapade he had bounced me up and down on his knees and said, 'I'm going to love and look after this little girl as though she is my very own.' It was a scene I so often pictured, me with the father I should have had. Instead we had been left with a memory of a much better time when all had seemed 'perfect' and everyone happy, an image that perhaps we both idealised.

At the top of the quartzite scree trail I reached a trig point, a distinctive concrete pillar once used by surveyors, now often invaluable to walkers finding their way. When I looked back, Frank was no longer in view. I could see that a sharp, rocky ridge rose higher on my right, so I realised that the summit was further still. The others were going to take ages, so I thought I'd attempt the file-edged route to the mountain's top. My stomach fluttered as an unstable rock shifted when I stood on it. Maybe it had been the earlier sight of Liathach that had unnerved me, or maybe it was my lack of experience – I'd never been so high on any mountain, I was alone, it all seemed so precarious, and I suddenly felt vulnerable. Dropping onto my hands and knees, I crawled along until I decided to give up and return to the trig. There was still no sign of Frank, Irina or Roman, but, glad to be back on more stable ground, I bounced off over some rocks and ran along the next bit of ridge, where, finding a spot out of the wind, I sat and waited for them to catch up. Sitting there all alone I felt my insignificance, my own mortality next to the great ages of the rocks around me.

Frank came into sight. I waved and called out to him, pointing to the path that dropped down. 'Is this the way?'

He confirmed that it was so I carried on ahead. I made my way down to the col, the lowest point between the ridges. There was a lot of sandstone and quartzite, indented with curious circular designs, like the mark a pastry-cutter leaves in rolled dough. I was certain I was looking at the fossil of some ancient creature, that this rock held great secrets, and in that moment I felt a definite spiritual presence in nature. Fascinated, I picked up a small piece to carry home. As I held the rock I was aware of that same sense of history that I'd experienced inside the walls of Ryvoan bothy, except the stone I now had in my hand whisked my imagination away on a much grander timescale: a connection to a past from which we all come – and maybe, in a more basic sense, it reminded me that we all come from, and will return to, dust. I felt comforted by that thought and was so absorbed in the moment that I didn't notice that the others had caught up and now it was I who had been left behind.

The only way to the floor of the next corrie was to descend an incredibly steep and narrow scree gully. Keeping to the right, using the rock wall as a support, I made my way down the stony staircase while Frank, Irina and Roman were slip-sliding their way ahead. The sky above the col was a magnificent gentian blue, which deepened into darker hues as it edged towards outer space; what a great sense of peace I felt deep within right then.

Below the broken cliffs and beyond the scree gully were irregular-shaped boulders varying in size – picking a way over them felt interminable as I dropped down into the natural amphitheatre; it was truly impressive. Under the surveillance of the almost vertical triple buttresses on my left, their lower halves sandstone and upper sections shining quartzite, it almost felt as if I was trespassing. Then, unexpectedly revealing itself at the foot of the towering rocks was the most beautiful loch I'd ever seen; it was so close. Captivated by its shimmering, iridescent blue waters, I was transfixed.

While I was lost in thought I found myself squatting at the lochan's edge, enjoying the sensation of the icy water as it ran through my fingers and swallowed up my hot, sticky hands. That's when I noticed that the wind had dropped. Stillness: not a sound except for the gentle movement of the loch water as the exit stream found its way over rocks and plunged down the mountainside. I almost didn't dare breathe, as if doing so would shatter the silence commanded by the council of walls around me. I felt spooked and yet thoroughly enchanted in this peaceful place: these mountains were magical. It had definitely been a struggle to get here, but clearly it was worth it.

'*Things in general don't come easy, and achieving anything worth-while takes hard work and time*,' I said softly to myself, thinking not just of the trek up here but also how hard I was still finding it to live without my mum. I wondered if that was why she had carried on walking after Gerry had died, if it had been her way of coming to terms with her own grief.

After Gerry's death there were reminders of him and what my mother had lost everywhere. Redundant wedding invitations lay stacked in a neat pile on the kitchen table, never to be posted. The service at the Garrison chapel and reception at Cameron Barracks had to be cancelled. The dining room was full of cases of champagne, and the wedding dress that Mum had been in the process of making was spread over the table, along with an embroidery she was sewing to give to Gerry on their wedding day, its words now taking on new meaning: *Today is the First Day of the Rest of Your Life*. And then, the most heartbreaking reminder of all – a letter arrived from him, written shortly before he died.

Camp I – 17,000 feet 24th April

My Dear Jenny,
Wonderful to hear from you again – I received your two let-ters of the 10th and 16th together, to-day. Particularly for the 16th that's fast going to this remote camp on the glacier. I was interested to hear that the material for your wedding dress has come through – you say it's lovely but tell me what colour it

is and whether it is plain or patterned? The weather with you sounds rather unpleasant – I heard through a fellow member that London also experienced snowfalls over Easter. I'm sure with the clothing you wear to work that you are far worse off than me. We have just experienced another fairly heavy snowfall but the worst aspect of the climate are the very chill winds. To-day the upper air-stream is moving along at 100mph and it's blowing from Siberia and Tibet.

You wouldn't recognise me at present – shaggy, unkempt hair, straggly beard and moustache, peeling nose and split lips – still love me!? Oh, and my teeth haven't been cleaned for a month: my tent companion tells me I look better than I did! I'm going to have to watch him. Seriously I'm looking anxiously to the day when I can once more set my eyes on you – it doesn't seem so far away now.

Our return trip to the UK looks a little unsettled but I'm still fairly confident that I should get back by the end of the first week of June.

Tell your mum, that instead of going on the Aberdeen trip, to join me here – the altitude and exercise reduces you to a scarecrow in no time despite eating twice the amount you normally do at home!

Tomorrow I'm off to Camp II at 19,000 feet. It's a delightful campsite, set on a ridge. The early morning sun soon reaches it and the views are fantastic. However, the day's work will consist of humping 40lb loads up to 20,000 feet. Needless to say, my love, I miss you very much.

All my love as ever, Gerry xxx

On the day my mother should have married Gerry my gran invited a small gathering of close friends for a lavish lunch. The idea was to cheer her daughter up and take her mind off the day. Steaming food was brought to the dining table and laid out so that everyone could serve themselves, while Uncle Jimmy was asked to open a bottle of the champagne that had been destined for the wedding. As he pushed, the cork gave way under pressure of the bubbles inside and unexpectedly flew out from the bottle's neck and smashed into the chandelier. Droplets of glass shattered into tiny sparkling shards, falling like a shower of diamonds all over the food. Amid gasps, a heavy chair scraped across the wooden floor as Mum withdrew from the table and fled from the room in tears.

The gloomy atmosphere prevailed within the walls of Inchrye for a long time. Unspeakable grief consumed my mother. She barely uttered a single word for over six months. She wrote poems for no one to read and would disappear on long, solitary walks for hours on end. Nobody could get through to her, not even me. Grandad would go to work with a heavy heart as he worried over his daughter, while Gran attended to mundane rituals of house-keeping and looking after everyone. Like the grown-ups, I got on with each day in my own way, roaming around the house or playing in the garden; but underneath the surface was a different matter. I was insecure, my mum was distant and I was too young to understand why.

Mum eventually forced herself to get on with her life without Gerry and completed a four-year teacher-training course. There were a few boyfriends over the years and I resented them all – they just weren't Gerry.

Then Mum met Frank. He and my uncle David had served in the same regiment since the late 1970s and the pair had frequently come to Inchrye when they were both on leave. Mum's new career took the two of us to Nairn, and since my grandparents were getting older, and Inchrye was far too large for just the two of them, they sold up and also moved to the town. But instead of going to their bungalow, Frank would come to visit Mum and me in our tiny home.

In the beginning I didn't mind – he was just my uncle's fun friend who always brought me sweets and junk; we used to play cards and he'd let me win his money, I loved hearing his rude jokes and his crazy, infectious laugh. But then I began to notice he was spending more and more time with us and it didn't take too much longer before I worked out that there was something going on between my mum and him.

It was 1984 and I was about to enter those hideously awkward years: the teens. The timing was bad, although to be fair he stood little chance of winning me round anyway. There hadn't been anyone on the scene for a few years, not since Mum's college days, and I'd been used to having her to myself. I didn't want this guy muscling in, stealing her affection from me. Up till now I'd accepted that she was busy with school work and I had been content to play quietly with my dolls while she sat doing her planning and marking. I accepted the fact that she had to work and wasn't bothered that she didn't give me her full attention, but now here he was, and she was giving him her time. I felt jealous of him and unimportant to her, and I behaved horrifically, making their every attempt at a private life impossible. Neither of them deserved the teenage tantrums, but no matter how vile I was, Frank showed great understanding. He was the one who came into the bedroom I shared with Mum to sit with me when I was sleep-talking – well, he said it was more like sleep-yelling. He could be good-natured, kind and caring. But, being too immature, I took no notice of these qualities.

I continued to resent his relationship with my mother. In the flat, when Frank and Mum weren't paying attention, I'd hide his cigarettes one by one: subtle and highly irritating. And when he returned to duty in Northern Ireland I would wiggle the connection from the phone just enough so that it looked like it was still plugged in. Sometimes Mum didn't notice for days. After a year the strain of a long-distance relationship, coupled with my adolescent outbursts, became too much. I found a letter Frank had sent to Mum, in which he'd written, 'can't you see the beauty of her love for you?' and added that he was prepared to 'weather the storm'. But Mum called the relationship off.

My mum never once blamed me, not to my face anyway. And though at the time I was glad Frank was gone and that I had Mum back to myself, I did feel guilty and responsible for their split. It wasn't good to feel that I had caused Mum such deep misery that she had sacrificed her own happiness for mine.

After ten years they eventually got back together again. They got married, too, but they were only man and wife for three months before cancer took her life. Their marriage ceremony in the chapel at Fort George was both joyful and sad. At the reception afterwards we toasted what was meant to be one of the happiest days of their lives when Grandad presented Mum with a bottle of champagne – one he had held on to for a long time: it was the very last of those bought to celebrate Mum's wedding to Gerry twenty-two years earlier, and now, at last, it would be opened. Mum passed me a champagne flute. I raised it to my lips but the lump in my throat made it hard to swallow the fizzy liquid. How could I pretend to be happy when I knew the reason she'd got married was because time was running out? In 1975 it had been her tears falling into the glass, in 1997 the tears were mine.

The wind suddenly kicked up and ripped through the stillness like the invasion of a school playground at the sound of the three o'clock bell, blowing the water back up the waterfall. Frank, Irina and Roman were still labouring over the boulders, so to kill some time I walked out on the stalkers' path, pausing to watch three deer, one posed majestically as if for a photograph. When they finally trotted off, I retraced my steps back up to the loch. There they were. I was starting to feel a bit irate at all the delays, but then Frank revealed the surprise.

'Well,' he said, 'that's the end of phase three. Don't you know where you are?'

I had a think but shook my head.

'The last time we tried to come here you were four months pregnant. The time before that was with Mum.'

It all came flooding back. This was the loch at Coire Mhic Fhearchair, a place Mum had wanted to visit ever since Frank had shown her photos of one of his trips here. As she became sicker it seemed increasingly important to her that she do it, and so the three of us attempted it just a couple of months before her death.

She had convinced herself, and us, that she was fit enough for the walk, but when we were a little over halfway to the loch she'd had to call it a day. Mum really wasn't well and, although disappointed she hadn't made it to the loch he especially wanted to share with her, Frank knew we absolutely had to turn back and get Mum home – and he was with her every step of the way.

We had tried to return, Frank and I, on Valentine's Day 1998, six months after Mum died. But I was carrying an already large pregnant bump and it had been my turn to struggle. The winding trail felt interminable as I trailed far behind Frank, and as the wind battered around the side of Sail Mhor it took my breath away. It was madness to try to carry on – and I too had had to give up. I yelled, hoping Frank would hear my voice over the wind. He did. I felt bad for him as we walked back. I understood that he'd wanted to come here to remember Mum. To relive the walk we'd done just months earlier with her at our side; we both needed to feel that connection to her. Twice we'd been on Beinn Eighe, and twice we'd turned back before reaching the loch. Now we'd finally made it, and it felt like Mum was here with me.

Inhaling deeply, I stood still for a few moments absorbing views of the wild, ragged landscape. Standing in that space of irresolution I felt entirely at the mercy of the mountain: and there was something strangely reassuring about that.

CHAPTER FOUR

Cheating Myself

Ben Wyvis — The Hill of Terror, July 2008

O n Ben Wyvis the cloud can settle on the top and clear up again many times in one day. I knew that well from all the years I had spent staring out of our second-floor kitchen window. With the naked eye, on a clear day I could see over the outer Moray Firth, all the way along the coastline from nearby Black Isle and Cromarty to as far up as Caithness — probably about forty miles away as the crow flies. It was a far less hilly view than the one I'd enjoyed from the old family home in Ardersier, but while Ben Wyvis was the only proper mountain I had a glimpse of from here, I loved being able to see for miles around me.

So I knew that what happened at the top on any given day was always hit or miss, but as I looked over blue-slate rooftops, the church spire and the water, the weather seemed fair and the mountain cloud-free. I decided it was a fine day to go up the Ben. And I'd been itching to take my boys up their first Munro, as any mountain in Scotland over 914 metres is known.

Marcus and Leon were like chalk and cheese, both in looks and personality; aged nine, Marcus was dark-haired with hazel eyes, while seven-year-old Leon was my fair-haired, blue-eyed boy. Where Marcus would be content to play quietly, Leon was a rascal. They even expressed affection differently, especially when they were tots: where Marcus would offer a gentle cuddle Leon would come running at me, deliver a swift blow to whichever of my body parts he came into contact with first, then growl, 'I LOVE YOU MUMMY!'

I'd already taken them out with me on many long walks and I'd recently started to introduce them to the hills as well, tackling Meall a' Bhuachaille with them. Now I felt they were ready for their first big climb, hoping that the mountains would bring us closer together, just as walking had with me and my mother. But it turned out that none of us was quite prepared for what was waiting for us on their first Munro.

Ben Wyvis was about an hour's drive from home, and the circuitous route I'd picked from my book had suggested the walk would only take around six to eight hours. I was feeling confident and well prepared when we set out walking along the well-constructed path, glad to be with the two little humans who meant most in the world to me. As we walked up through trees and enjoyed views of the river racing and frothing over rocks on our right, the sun's warmth was delicious as it beat down. The straps of my overstuffed daysack rubbed against the exposed flesh of my shoulders, but I felt too content to care as I enjoyed watching my boys happily exploring, Marcus staying close by while Leon made straight for a small burn that dissected the path to poke at some water spiders. But as we continued into more open land, the weather changed all too quickly.

Patches of cloud blotted out the sun, and the wind suddenly blew harder, making it feel considerably colder. I was glad I'd had the foresight to pack extra clothing for us all, which we threw on, halfway up, by the shelter of a camper-van-sized rock. Our cheerful mood soon evaporated, replaced by a steady stream of moans and groans, mostly falling from Leon's lips. At the height of his disenchantment he declared crossly this was 'a wasted day' and 'a meaningless walk to the top of a lump of earth', which despite everything made me laugh, and he soon saw the funny side too.

It really was a hard slog for untrained calf muscles, though, as we continued upwards. The path edged the mountainside and it was a long drop down. In a reversal of roles, Marcus appeared to be in his element, much more confident and adventurous, whereas Leon seemed to have lost his usual fearless approach to life and was demonstratively ill at ease when he saw his brother investigating a large, flat slab of rock, like a shelf, jutting out over the valley below.

'Tell him to come back, Mummy! He'll get blown off the mountain!' Leon wailed.

I reassured my younger son as he clutched my hand tightly, though in truth I'd been watching his brother with nervous pride myself. I called Marcus to rejoin us, and he immediately scrabbled back before forging off ahead once more.

'Auch, man, you have got to be kidding me!' he called back.

Laughing, I realised he must have reached a false summit. After battling up heathery slopes we were fully exposed as we topped out onto a dirtied-amber flat-summit skyline, and the wind buffeted around us mercilessly. We gazed down upon views of the Cromarty and Moray Firths, steely grey waters spilling from their triangular inlets into the expanse of the North Sea, which filled the horizon. It was tremendous to be so high up. To see so far out into watery nothingness in one direction, and in the other to behold an inanimate world of seemingly endless peaks fading into the distance. I hoped the boys shared my sense of awe.

The going was now easier as we tramped across woolly hair moss over the broad ridge, but we were still just over a kilometre and a half away from the summit. We watched as cloud drifted onto, over the top of, and away again from Ben Wyvis's highest point. The boys were delighted by large pockets of snow still clinging to the deep, craggy corrie on our right, but I began to worry about the deteriorating weather closing in around us. It was one thing to watch weather fold and unfold from my kitchen window, but to be right here experiencing it in the fabric of the landscape, on the peak of this big, rolling, fuck-off mountain, was something completely different.

At the shelter cairn we huddled together, seeking extra protection from the wind behind the concrete trig point. Dense mists surrounded us and, as my shivering boys ate their sandwiches, a sense of irresponsibility rolled about my stomach in sickening waves.

I stared at the drawing of the route I'd printed from the Munro book realising, with growing fright, how redundant it was without a proper OS map. It was wildly less than adequate for the zero-visibility conditions we were now in. We were only at the halfway point. I'd thought we'd be much further along by now and would easily beat any change in the weather. Of course, I'd anticipated it would take longer with two small kids in tow than if I'd been on my own, but now I realised I'd vastly underestimated just how much longer. Now I was up here in bad weather with my children, frightened and out of my depth. But panicking in front of the boys was not an option. I just needed to think.

I figured there were three choices: stay put and hope the weather cleared up again before we all froze to death; try to continue following our planned route despite no longer having a clear idea of where that was; or return the way we'd come, hoping we'd be able to retrace our steps and keep to the path. It wasn't a happy situation – two options carried a high risk of getting lost, and in all three there was a chance we could end up with hypothermia. As I sat shivering next to my boys, my terrified mind began to play out the tragic scene of our deaths, and then of my own death in which my children were left without their mother. I didn't want them to have to grow up without me: it had been bad enough losing my own mum at twenty-four; they were far too young to go through that sort of pain and suffering. Who would look after them if I was gone? Those thoughts made me pull myself together with a firm resolve. They were not going to die today, and neither was I.

I was twenty-one years old when I'd arrived back in the country on 18 December 1993 after spending two weeks in Thessaloniki, Greece. It was quite late, after I'd caught various buses from Aberdeen airport, when I opened the door to my wee student bedsit on Hardgate. Despite the hour, I phoned home to wish my grandad a happy eightieth birthday.

'I think you'd better give your mum a call, Sarah, pet,' he said.

My mum had been diagnosed with breast cancer.

'I've had lumps before, but they were just cysts. I went into the doctor's once with one and came out with five,' she said.

It felt like I was falling in spirals from a great height as my stomach dropped and churned. She was only forty. A stabbing pain clawed across my chest.

'I'm gonna get the first bus home,' I told her.

Mum's next appointment was on the Monday and I went with her to the hospital.

'And you've had this lump for about a year?' the doctor enquired.

'Yes . . . I didn't get checked for so long because the lump is the antithesis of what my local GP advised me to look out for,' she answered defensively. 'It's wiggly and mobile. I assumed it was another cyst.'

Mum was admitted for a lumpectomy and discharged from hospital on Christmas Eve.

'I feel exhausted,' she said, and then she cried.

Days passed in a numb blur until the college holidays were coming to a close.

'My radiotherapy sessions start on 7 January. Least I'll get a whole term off school,' Mum told me.

'Do you want me to stay home. I can help you?' I offered. I didn't want to leave her to deal with this on her own, I wanted to be there for her – and I wanted her to want me to be there for her.

'Thank you, Sarah, but no. There's nothing you can do. The treatment only lasts six weeks and then that's it. I just want everything to carry on as normal, so you get back to art school,' she answered affectionately.

She still looked and sounded like my mum, yet cancer, this hateful disease, seemed to have lodged itself between us. Now she felt more distant than ever. She was probably trying to protect me by sending me away, but at the time I only saw it as rejection. I couldn't help my mum. I was utterly powerless, still cartwheeling from the sky. It felt like it didn't matter what I did; the sick in my guts and fog in my head were there to stay.

Maybe it was that feeling of rejection, combined with the fear that I might lose her, that caused me to suddenly rebel. In the following weeks and months my life slid out of control quite quickly. Shopping sprees became opportunities to thieve out of devilment rather than need, and I was drinking more than was good for me. I loved painting in my studio, sometimes staying late till only the cleaners were around, but when my day at college was through I found myself getting either stoned, pissed or both. Weekends extended, beginning on a Thursday and ending on a Monday, and if Kate, my only friend at college, was preoccupied with her boyfriend then I'd go out alone, latching on to anybody in the various bars and clubs I frequented.

Bad dreams disturbed my sleep, ones in which I had only days to live because it was me who had cancer, not Mum. And then there were night terrors – the paradox of knowing I was asleep, but believing I was awake. In these episodes I could see my soul extricating itself, taking flight from my lifeless corpse. In others the Devil himself was coming for me. He'd be outside my window ready to get in and I, by some supernatural force, found myself crawling, as though through treacle, on hands and knees across the ceiling, desperately making a bid for freedom. There was no respite from Mum's cancer. No escape.

I was drinking so much that blackouts were becoming a common occurrence, but I started passing out too. I was swinging on a chair at the Students' Union one minute and the next everything went black. It wasn't until the very end of the night that the people I was with got me to my feet and helped me to leave. If I was still conscious at closing time I'd try to find a party, just to keep pouring down the alcohol. Sometimes I'd make it back to my bedsit and not remember how, but more often home was a distance too far so I'd crash out wherever I ended up.

The boys next door weren't exactly a stabilising influence. They'd already shown me how to identify which mushrooms were the magic ones, but tripping out, I discovered, was definitely not for me.

'Why don't you just stick to blow?' my neighbour's muffled voice said before he inhaled deeply, while his flatmate, having drawn on a loaded joint, blew its smoke up through the black pipe attached to the mask on my friend's face. Pale features, framed by his ginger locks and black rubber, disappeared in a fog behind the clear plastic visor and I laughed when he re-emerged looking an even more ghostly white, his eyes glazed, totally stoned. It was my turn to pull on the gas mask and take a blow back through the concertinaed hose. But it wasn't enough for me; I was going out to the pub in case I missed out – on what, I don't know – and so I left them with their mask and blow in their squalid rented room. I passed out that night too. I didn't register what was at the root of my behaviour so I did nothing to break the pattern, not even when the events of a night out turned a shade darker.

I'd switched on the TV, browsing through channels to figure out if it was afternoon or early morning. It wasn't great that I'd lost a day at college, but on the bright side I didn't have to wait long to go to the pubs. I thought alcohol made me happy and gave me confidence. But there I was, alone again, in a booth at the Students' Union, all maudlin and introspective. I phoned my neighbour to tell him I felt suicidal. He had come more than once to get me, but on this occasion it was a mutual friend who turned up – someone I fancied – and took me home. One minute we were kissing on the sofa, the next he'd pushed me to the floor and was forcing himself on me. It was over within minutes. He readjusted himself and left. I sat staring at the blurry vision of my jeans around my knees. I remained there for a moment in a state of total confusion before cleaning myself up and crawling into bed. What I should have done was call the police, but I didn't – because I'd invited him in and had enjoyed him pressing his lips to mine, and because my efforts to fend him off when he pushed me down consisted of two alcohol-weakened hands pressed flat against his chest until I gave up and let him get on with it, and because I was so drunk. He'd physically hurt me, but I blamed myself entirely. I felt shame, too much to be able to tell anyone. And I felt worse than ever before.

While I was busy screwing myself up, Mum's treatment had been hard going for her.

'How are you feeling?' I asked when I called home.

'Glad the radiotherapy is over. I felt so sick and lethargic all the time. I've had enough of hospital and doctor appointments. I just want to get on with things now.'

'So the cancer is all gone?'

'Yes. The doctor said I'll have to go for check-ups, but after five years I should get the all-clear.'

It was a relief to hear her airy optimism, and so I buried my fears.

Summer term had come round and I threw myself into the routine of art school. I was relieved that the doctors had dug out and zapped Mum's cancer, but I remained unsettled. I began a secret affair with one of the visiting tutors. He was married. It was clandestine, and I enjoyed it. I grew fond of him because he seemed to genuinely care, and he was gentle with me. But the affair was almost as though I was substituting one bad habit for another. Like alcohol and shoplifting, he was the initial high of those first few drinks, and the buzz I felt at getting away with thieving. My satiation was only ever temporary. It was like I was addicted to danger and unpredictability. Eventually our involvement, just like my worst hangovers, made me feel regret and shame. He wasn't mine to have and so we came to an end. As usual, I promised myself that I'd change, that I'd be better.

With the degree show only weeks away, I needed to make new plans and decided the best thing would be to get as far away as possible from Aberdeen – even from Scotland. I applied for a postgraduate place at a quaint and ramshackle art college in a small village called Lemba, several miles from Paphos on the Greek side of Cyprus. I wanted Mum to think that I was taking responsibility for my future; I didn't want her to worry about me.

Six months later I was living in Cyprus, I had a boyfriend and was feeling good. I thought I had things under control. But I was kidding myself. A couple of months later my boyfriend dumped me. What he had first been attracted to in my crazy, drunken behaviour had become a worry and burden.

'You can't just enjoy one or two drinks, you always have to get fucking trashed,' he said. 'I'm fed up of all your moaning and feeling sorry for yourself. I've had enough.'

Feeling lonely and discarded, I went even wilder than I had been in Aberdeen. Craving attention, I went on benders and would sing and dance on tables. I skinny-dipped in the sea under a full moon. I got so drunk I thought I was lost in a jungle, when really I was on the terrace outside my room. Twice in one night I was found asleep and snoring in the middle of the road behind our accommodation block, and I'd wake up in other people's rooms, wondering how I'd got there. In the dead of night I'd ridden off on my moped, blazing drunk and high on grass, determined to find someone to party with. And in the morning, still under the influence, I rode off to work without realising I was missing the left lens of my sunglasses. I was a danger, and a mindless idiot. Christ, I even called the Mayor of Nicosia the 'c' bomb before I did a bunk with one of the diplomats: it was meant to be a laugh.

The confidence and impulsiveness that drink gave me to go up and talk to strangers made me come across as annoying, and often my ambition to seek comfort ended up as a fleshy encounter.

Hungover, I'd hide in my studio space by day, my stomach seizing when people came to tell me what I'd done or whom I'd pissed off.

I made plenty of excuses to myself for my loose and chaotic behaviour. But every situation I found myself in was of my own making, and I alone was responsible for the fact I was becoming less likeable with each passing day. I'd stretched the limits of the relationship I'd had – and common decency – like a rubber band because I'd lost myself in drink. I didn't want to be that person. I needed to go back home, promising myself once more I would be better.

When I returned home from Cyprus, hoping to make another fresh start, it was Mum who helped put me back on track. She let me use one of the smaller rooms in our flat as a studio, and supported me financially until I found work, at first in a bar and then running a local art gallery. I was even getting on well with Frank, who by this time was back on the scene. A relatively harmonious and productive year soon passed. Life had settled.

It was mid August 1996 and I'd just completed a series of sea and landscape paintings for exhibition at a small London gallery. The next morning, I heard Mum talking on the phone to Gran.

'I've got an appointment with the doctor at two o'clock,' she said.

Our year of peace had been the calm before the storm.

After Mum's appointment with the doctor she was admitted to hospital. At ten-thirty the next morning she called.

'The CT scan revealed a tumour on my brain. It's small, easily accessible and they're going to be able to remove it.' Her words were a dizzying drug flooding my body from head to toe, but I understood what they meant. She had secondary cancer: ultimately, a death sentence.

'I'm coming in with Gran and Grandad, we'll be there soon. Have you told Frank?' I asked. After he and my uncle David came out of the army they'd gone into business together. He was away working on a removal job in London and wasn't due home for two more days.

'No. There's no point. There isn't anything he can do, it can wait till he's back,' she answered. My grandparents and I arrived at the hospital to see Mum, and each of us kept our feelings in check. 'I've just had a chest X-ray and tomorrow I'm getting a scan on my liver and bones to make sure that no spores have manifested there,' she said.

The situation was surreal, like the bad dreams I used to have. Conversation was stilted small talk that none of us had any real interest in, but better that than loaded silence. We all wanted out of there, we had all wanted to wake up from the nightmare.

Back at my grandparents' house I took the dog's lead and stuffed biscuits into my jacket pocket. 'C'mon, Poppy. Walkies,' I called. Ears pricking, she got up from her basket and crossed the kitchen, her wagging tail and a lick of my hand indicating she was ready to go. She was a faithful and gentle old girl, a cross between a Labrador and a lurcher. She had been part of our family since she was a pup, rescued from the needle two nights before Remembrance Sunday by my grandad. A myriad of thoughts thumped in my head. Both Poppy and I wanted the freedom of the wide open space offered by the beach: she so that she could chase gulls and I hoping the sea breeze would blow all the upset and pain away. I turned at the kitchen door before I left.

'Do you believe in God, Grandad?' I asked.

'If only I knew the answer, Sarah pet. It's something I've often asked myself, but I do think all this can't be here just by chance.'

My grandad was the smartest man I knew; he could speak a number of languages fluently, and I was always impressed that he could do the *Telegraph* cryptic crossword puzzle. I thought he had the answers to everything, but he couldn't tell me this. I decided that if God was there, then I was going to talk to Him more because my mum was not allowed to die.

The following day the four of us once again sat in the hospital's day room. 'The bone and liver scan were clear,' Mum announced. The news was a small lift. Things seemed even more hopeful when a member of nursing staff popped in to say the chest scan had been clear too – so it came as a shock to discover later that day that the nurse had made a terrible mistake. Three tumours were found on both lungs. 'Life will never be the same again,' Mum said quietly.

Within two weeks of the discovery of Mum's brain tumour the neurosurgeon had carried out a craniotomy at Aberdeen Royal Infirmary. When Mum came round from the anaesthetic she saw me standing at her side, and, breaking into sobs, raised a hand to her eyes. I leant forward and gently kissed her cheek. 'I love you too,' she whispered. Though she'd written those words in letters and cards, I couldn't remember the last time she'd come straight out and said them to me. My heart ached. She had once said that I shouldn't need to be told I was loved constantly – I should just know. I did know, of course I did, but sometimes I just needed the reassurance of hearing it. I suppose she did not always understand me and neither did I always understand her; it was only when I became a mother myself that I came to realise this is probably often the way with parents and their children.

Three days later Mum was discharged; however, she still had to face two weeks of radiotherapy. Sickness and lethargy that she knew was caused by the treatment returned. Mostly she just wanted to be by herself.

I took Poppy for long walks around the river and along the beach, my mind trying to process the inevitable truth that Mum was going to die. Everything seemed back to front: my grieving had already begun yet she was still alive, and any time we had left was destroyed by knowing that she would soon leave me for ever. Standing on a bridge, I felt tears roll off my cheeks. I cried in bed at night too, and voices inside my head would contradict each other. *I'm allowed to cry! But you shouldn't. You should be happy your Mum is still here. You should be enjoying the time you have left. Save your tears till after she's gone. I don't want her to go. That's why I'm crying.*

Dreams were full of images in which my mum was suffering, shrieking in pain, and always I looked on helplessly. Mum's cancer and its consequences remained dark, amorphous beasts, lingering and unshifting in my mind.

I'd spent many afternoons painting. It was normally an absorbing activity, but now I couldn't concentrate. Abandoning my task, I lay on top of my bed crying silently, tears gathering in tickly pools inside my ears. As if she had somehow sensed my distress, Mum came to my room and sat on the edge of the bed.

'It looks like you're suffering more than I am,' she said as she stroked my hair.

'I love you. I don't want you to die,' I blurted selfishly, crying even harder. Her voice soothed me as she told me to let it all out.

'Everyone has to die; it's the one and only guarantee in life. And when I'm gone of course you will cry. Give yourself a couple of weeks, but then I want you to get on with your life; just keep busy,' she said.

Mum always found the right words to say, maybe that's why she had always seemed old to me. But at forty-three she was only a young woman herself, and I think maybe now she needed me as much as I did her.

Like most parents, all I wanted was to provide better everything for my children, but I constantly felt a sense of inadequacy. And I wondered what chance they had of growing up to be happy and secure when their mother was neither of these things. Now on the summit of Ben Wyvis, as the self-flagellation continued, I worried alone, my mind replaying fragments of an old conversation:

'What will I do when you're not here, Mum, and I have an important decision to make and need your advice?'

'You'll just have to try and imagine what I would say.'

I was contemplating the best course of action when out from the thick furls of white mists a lone walker appeared. He was a young lad in his early twenties and without much mountain experience himself; he didn't have a map or compass, but he did have a GPS. Between us we managed to navigate the rest of the circuitous route together and at quarter past seven in the evening, after nine hours of walking, my boys and I were reunited with the car. The boys greeted our black carriage home with an abundance of kisses to its windows. They were shattered but had been completely oblivious to the dangers we had faced, while I was now flooded with relief at the happy outcome of what had been a fairly scary day: the hill of terror, so aptly named, had taught me my toughest hillwalking lessons to date. Even in summer months the weather on the Scottish hills can be less than hospitable; print outs from my book did not in any acceptable way constitute a map; and, most importantly, I never ever wanted to put my boys in harm's way again because of my ignorance.

Yet there was still so much more for me to learn.

CHAPTER FIVE

Becoming a Woman with a Plan

Beinn Alligin — The Jewelled Hill, August 2008

I n the couple of months since I had been on Beinn Eighe in
Wester Ross with Frank, things at home with Sam had been
going increasingly downhill. Drink was the wedge that continued to drive us apart bit by bit. I didn't look forward to weekends
in particular. We argued constantly. I tried various tactics to
avoid confrontation, from sneaking off to bed and pretending I
was asleep to buying a karaoke machine, but still it felt as though
there was no escape from it. Sometimes it went on all night, until it
was light outside, and I was so sleep deprived I no longer felt able
to function as a normal human being, or as a mother. Thankfully
the boys seemed to be unaware of how badly our relationship had
deteriorated. But still we remained together. I didn't want to fail.
I didn't want to lose my husband.

Adding to life's daily stresses — my deteriorating marriage,
balancing work and children, arranging repairs caused by a leaking roof — nine people now lodged in the flat opposite, and the
building's plumbing system couldn't cope. Pipes would block and

stink us out and our water supply was drawn away by a pump they'd had installed, leaving us with not so much as a droplet in our taps – ironic when they then flooded us.

I needed to get out on the hills again.

I decided to return to Wester Ross, this time to climb Beinn Alligin, another one of the Torridonian giants. These mountains form a dramatic landscape, their peaks rising up sheer from the sea. In comparison with its neighbours, Beinn Eighe and the mighty Liathach, Beinn Alligin is the easiest of the Torridon ridge traverses, but it includes a series of three towering rock pinnacles known as the Horns, and covering all of them would involve some exhilarating and airy scrambling.

Recent weather had been untypical of our rainy Scottish summers and an area of high pressure brought settled weather over the country. After the recent experience on Ben Wyvis with my children, I felt much happier to be venturing out under clearer skies, and I felt more confident having already done this walk a couple of weeks earlier.

The memory of our long day on Ben Wyvis was too raw for Leon, and though I tried to sell the walk as being 'only half the distance' and 'not as high', he emphatically declared he was not coming. But Marcus, enthused by the description I'd given of scrambling over the Horns, keenly agreed to accompany me.

We arrived at the small car park off the road to Diabaig at the back of Torridon House around ten o'clock the next morning. As we tramped across moorland it was much drier underfoot than the squelchy conditions I'd encountered on the walk previously; it had been a clammy day then, with no wind or rain, and views had been obscured by low cloud before the corrie headwall had even been reached.

What a contrast now as Marcus and I sweated under the heat of the sun, up the steepening path that zigzagged into the corrie. I puffed and panted as I toiled uphill, not talking because I was breathing so hard, but Marcus was a mountain goat, only stopping in his tracks to look at frogs or dragonflies and to stare out a grasshopper with its giant, red eyes. Marcus had his father's looks, but his inherent gentle nature and placid disposition reminded me so much of my mum. He was turning out to be the best of both his dad and me.

I had never wanted either of my boys to grow up without a dad, like I had. When I'd got involved with each of their fathers, it was with the expectation that we'd stay together, but neither relationship had worked out. I was grateful that Marcus had a positive rapport with his father. I just wished Leon got to see more of his dad, but at least there was contact from time to time. My natural father had abandoned me completely from the start.

I did eventually meet him. I don't really know what I had been expecting, but still the encounter was a let-down.

It was a Sunday morning in 1989. I was seventeen and still dozing in bed when Mum came into my room.

'Sarah, your father's here,' she said. The news came as a complete surprise. Only a week or so earlier I'd asked Mum about my real dad, and she'd asked if I wanted to meet him. I had said I did, but I'd never imagined our first encounter could come about so quickly.

My emotions were all mixed up. He'd been living nearby all this time, and my mum had clearly had no difficulty in getting hold of him. *If it was that easy to have got in touch why is it only now that he is here? Why has he never wanted to see me before now?*

I was angry that he'd abandoned us – run a mile from his responsibilities as soon as he'd got Mum pregnant, back to the wife he'd previously denied existed. But I was also curious about this man. And nervous to finally meet him. I was a little afraid my mum would feel upset that I had brought him back into her life; I didn't want her to think I was being disloyal – she was the most important person to me, I hoped she knew that.

With nervous apprehension I got up, pulled on some clothes and went to the living room. There he was, dressed in a grey suit that had a sheen to it, sitting on our sofa; his hair was thick and his beard well groomed and the colour of autumn leaves. His eyes were big and round with long lashes – like mine. The atmosphere was awkward, but he tried to make an effort.

A few days later he took me to Dingwall, a small town fifteen minutes north of Inverness, where he was opening a new nightclub. We went in his flashy white BMW and had a wander around the club. On its wall was a badly painted mural of singing legends.

He was all chuffed and asked, 'What do you think?' and 'Do you like the dance floor?'

'I do,' I said. It was made up of squares that flashed different colours in sync with the music. I liked his car too. But I didn't want to like him.

On the third and final time we met he took my mum and me out for dinner and gave me *The Lost Boys* video. He said he'd like to get a phone installed at our home, so that he could get in touch more easily and get to know me better, but Mum later told me it was so he could arrange to see her. What a prick. I felt hurt and unimportant and more confused than ever. And so I sent him a vicious letter, writing that I hoped he'd be repaid with the same humiliation he'd put my mother through when he'd denied both of us all those years ago. I was so angry, I cut him dead. I never heard from him again.

I was twenty-three when a call came through to the art college's office in Cyprus, where I was living at the time. Mum's voice was clear and unbroken at the end of the line.

'Mike's dead.'

'Who's Mike?'

'Your dad.'

'Oh . . . Right . . . What happened?' I asked, as a cocktail of horror, guilt and a tinge of remorse flooded through me like a numbing wave of morphine without the high.

'He died choking on his own vomit. He'd been at a party.' There was silence down the wires, I had no idea how to respond. Luckily my mother understood. 'You were never given the chance to develop any feelings of affection for your father,' she said. 'It's only natural you wouldn't feel the grief.' She was right: the man had only been my father in the most basic, biological sense – I couldn't cry or grieve for someone I never really knew. But the news still made me feel strange.

It was twilight as I made the solitary journey down the single-tracked military road, back to the whitewashed accommodation block and the sanctuary of my single room. Frogs in the valley were in full chorus. Soft pinks, orange and blue hues delicately wrapped themselves across the horizon joining sky and sea, and the remaining warmth of the day seemed to embrace me. As I walked I thought about what Mum had said and conversed silently with myself, batting statements and opinions back and forth like a game of ping-pong.

It's true. Mike has been absent my entire life – apart from those encounters when I was seventeen. Yes, and even then that contact had been arranged at your request. I had just wanted to see what a man who could so readily shirk his responsibilities looked like. You already knew the kind of man he was. Actions speak louder than words! But part of me is him and now he is gone. I'll never have another chance to get to know him. Was that letter I wrote too harsh? Should I not have broken off contact then?

My thoughts were suddenly interrupted by a dreadful sound as old Sol, who lived in an adobe shack behind the block I stayed in, hawked up phlegm. He'd been blinded from years of drinking absinthe, nobody saw much of him, just a shuffling shape in the shadows of his overgrown garden. I closed the door to my room on the world outside. *If he had really wanted to know you, no matter how awful the things were that you had written in that letter, he would have kept on trying to win you over.* I struggled to shift the guilt I felt. Yet there was nothing to be done about either those words in my letter or the undeniable fact that he was now as dead as a door-nail. I would never get to know who that missing part of me was.

In the same way I had once used the bottle and blow to bury all the hurt, I now found salvation in the freedom of wide, open

spaces. Among mountains I enjoyed a natural high. And I wondered, momentarily, if it was a similar pain that my father had
tried to blot out when he chose to drink himself to death. He chose
drink and drugs. I had chosen to live, to find a more positive outlet
for my turmoil, and to be there for my sons.

As Marcus and I climbed out from the dark confines of the
corrie on Beinn Alligin and topped out onto a fairly flat plateau,
we were rewarded with sudden and extensive views over sparkling
waters to Skye, Harris and the low-lying profile of Lewis. We were
standing high on the north-western edge of Scotland, with nothing
between us and the islands of Skye and the Outer Hebrides, dark,
angular outlines across the Minch. Behind and now way below
us, Loch Torridon glinted in still, blue perfection. Rising steeply
above its southern shore stood Beinn Damh, smaller than its
neighbours but stark and prominent with endless peaks sweeping
gracefully away behind it. We couldn't help but keep stopping to
admire the grandeur – while also enjoying some respite from the
hot work. With a film of sweat across our foreheads we climbed
higher still to reach the first summit, where we had a well-earned
rest. We weren't even bothered by the flies that buzzed around us
as we ate some lunch. Liathach dominated our view to the east,
that intimidating yet fascinating terraced sandstone monster. And
behind us, almost five kilometres in length, was the rest of our
ridgewalk. After our break, still feeling the heat, I whipped off
my sweat-soaked vest before moving on.

We could admire our surroundings properly now, like a work
of art, the sandstone ridge gently curving in a serpentine line all
the way towards the second summit, Sgurr Mor, and beyond it

the Horns. We carefully descended the steep, narrow ridge and the rock felt warm against the palms of our hands as we lowered ourselves over awkward drops that presented a stretch too long for our legs. Being with Marcus, and given the combination of good weather, incredible scenery and the challenge of the terrain, I felt consumed by an enormous sense of joy, and it seemed no time before we'd reached the col between the two Munro tops – only to have to begin another steep climb upwards. After ascending a smaller top, to our right a fantastically dramatic gash – the Eag Dubh gully – split the ridge. We paused momentarily to peer down and marvel at all the fallen rocks and rubble that had been weathered away and were now lying strewn on the corrie floor. I turned my face from the dark, shadowy confines of the gully and continued the trail, so brightly illumined in sunshine, to the height of Sgurr Mor. It felt good to be up here, to be part of nature's glorious mountain canvas. We'd done it together, me and my boy, and we couldn't stop grinning foolishly at each other, flushed with pleasure at our achievement.

From our second summit Liathach appeared even more imposing. My eyes remained transfixed on this isolated bastion with its precipitous walls. I knew one day I'd have to climb it, to satiate my curiosity. Beyond it were even more jagged tops. Land dressed in purple and deep-blue hues swept away into the distance to merge with the heated haze of the day and vastness of the sky, and I surrendered myself to the magic of the silence and beauty. Turning through 180 degrees, I gazed upon the Dundonnell and Fisherfield Hills, yawning off to the north. We sat quietly together, Marcus and I, tired but satisfied by the physical challenge.

We would have been content to stay there on the mountain's peak, but we still had to tackle the three pinnacles, so off we sauntered towards the Horns, with Beinn Dearg and Beinn Eighe as their backdrop. Scrambling over the airy sandstone towers held an attraction of its own. It was basically easy rock climbing and added an element of real fun to the day. Finding foot and hand holds with natural ease, Marcus scrambled up and down the rocky architecture of the Horns, loving every second of it. The warm wind blew more gustily, but, unfazed, he continued his route-finding with the utmost confidence, and his beaming smile as we arrived on the final pillar said more than the spoken word – almost.

'Can I call Dad?' he asked.

'Yeah, course you can,' I nodded, handing him my mobile.

'Dad was up here a few weeks ago, but he told me didn't manage the Horns because his legs were too tired for it. I can't wait to tell him I've done them,' he said gleefully.

'Dad! Guess where I am?' sang Marcus. 'I'm on the last Horn on Beinn Alligin.'

'Well done, Son,' I heard his father say, 'I'm going to have to attempt it again then.'

I'd met Marcus's dad in late autumn 1996, a couple of months after Mum's diagnosis. My moods had been low and so, in need of distraction, I had taken on extra evening shifts at the pub – and going by my track record it was far better that I was working and not drinking. It was there that I met the man who would father my first child. He looked like a young Charlie Sheen: his short, dark hair spiked at the front, almond-shaped green eyes and a perfectly proportioned, straight nose. He was interesting and as we chatted more I discovered he lived down the lane opposite Mum's flat, in a house tucked in behind high walls and trees next to the river. A whirlwind romance between us started out well and developed into a Christmas proposal of marriage at the summit of a local hill. But as months passed and my mum became sicker – more quickly than any of us thought possible – that whirlwind relationship creaked under the strain.

'Why is it that people always let you down and relationships end up pear-shaped? How am I going to live without you? It's always you I come to for advice. What is the point in anything!' I blurted as I approached my startled mother, who had been reading a book quietly by the fire.

'Oh Sarah, you must promise me that you won't give up,' Mum said as she stood up and held me to her.

'You're the only person I know I can trust,' I whined, as she stroked my hair and kept me in her arms. Just then my boyfriend walked into the room.

'You look after this girl,' Mum said to him. 'She's been starved of affection all her life.' We gently unlocked our embrace. My boyfriend looked suitably embarrassed, but I wasn't worried about him. All I could think about was how terrified I was to lose my mother from my life.

Coming off the final ridge felt rough on my knees, but I watched with pride as Marcus skipped and bounced his way downwards. Stopping in his flight, he turned to look at me, his face all tanned. 'Mum, I really enjoyed myself today,' he said. I beamed back, and with that he bounded off again. Marcus and I had always been close, and it was wonderful to be able to share these experiences with him.

Left alone with my thoughts for a moment, my mind wandered back to a conversation I'd had with a random stranger I'd walked this same bit of trail with weeks earlier.

'I want to climb Kilimanjaro. It's the highest free-standing mountain in Africa. It borders Tanzania and Kenya . . .' When he had said that I'd immediately thought of Mum. She had lived in Kenya as a kid. An idea started to take form.

As Marcus and I neared the bridge and the path that would return us to the car, I was convincing myself more and more that it should be me making the trip to Africa. If I felt released from the burden of my grief on the heathers and hills at home, maybe Kilimanjaro would expunge it for ever. I could climb that mountain as a personal tribute to Mum – and raise some money for charity too. It made sense.

'Hey, Mum,' Marcus called, breaking my train of thought. 'I found a stone and it's got a smiling face!' He pressed it into my hand; sure enough, iron oxide within the rock had created the illusion of two eyes and smile. Perceiving it as a good omen, I took it home as a reminder of our day. I was now a woman with a plan.

CHAPTER SIX

Divergent Paths

Meall Fuar-mhonaidh — The Cold Rounded Hill,
February 2010

My guidelines for life had always been the memories of conversations I'd had with Mum. *'Just keep busy!'* she had advised, and for the most part I had made sure I was occupied enough, always setting myself new goals. In 2008 I'd translated thought into action and signed up to join the Marie Curie Fundraising Team on their June 2010 Kilimanjaro trek. That gave me two years, the first to complete teaching probation and the second to fundraise.

Asking people for sponsorship was something I'd never been comfortable with, so I figured the best way to get people to part with money would be to run raffles at two dances I'd planned. I'd put all my energy into the project: sweet-talking local businesses for prizes in exchange for publicity on fliers, tickets and any newspaper articles that were published. People I didn't even know were kind and wanted to help. I'd been sponsored for all my trek clothing by an outdoors shop, all the tickets were printed by a proper printing press, gratis, and the upmarket hotel that gave me use of their dance hall also offered a weekend break as a raffle prize. And there were all sorts of other fabulous donations too: a helicopter flight, a large cash prize, various vouchers, a spa weekend – the list went on, and the generosity amazed me.

All that organisation had been difficult, but the real hard yards were selling the dance and raffle tickets – literally – as I knocked on almost every door in town, sometimes taking my children when I had nobody to look after them. But it was worthwhile because the townsfolk were big-hearted and we raised thousands of pounds for the charity.

With my hectic fundraising efforts over, I could turn my attention back to the main trouble in my life: my turbulent marriage. At the start of 2010, I finally made the decision it was over.

The final straw had been when Sam and I had taken the boys to Bulgaria for a skiing holiday over New Year. I'd wanted something we could all do together as a family, and I had hoped that skiing every day and sharing the same room with the boys would be just what we needed. It wasn't to be. Sam came up with a range of reasons as to why he couldn't ski: he'd left his jacket at home, his knees were hurting, he had a bad headache. Then came New Year. We enjoyed dinner and entertainment at our hotel then walked down to the main square in Bansko for midnight, where we set off sky lanterns. After a firework display we returned to the hotel. I took the boys to our mezzanine-style room, but Sam decided the night wasn't over and went back out. From experience, I knew this wasn't going to end well.

At seven-twenty on New Year's morning the sound of metal skittering off the edge of the hotel door lock alerted me to Sam's arrival. It took him ages to get the key into its hole and then several attempts to turn it the right way to open the door. In any other circumstances it would have been funny. He staggered in. Finally I heard him slump down onto one of the beds and the clickety-clack as the plastic ends of his laces bounced off the leather kilt shoes. Their untying was a battle more than he was capable of, and he cursed incomprehensibly in his Glaswegian accent before giving up and crashing out fully clothed. Snores to shake a continent were my cue to get up and leave. I woke the boys, we dressed quickly and quietly before creeping silently out of the room.

Walking along the empty streets of Bansko on that brisk and cold first day of 2010 was when I finally accepted that I was going to have to be brave and change my situation. This time, instead of making excuses to myself as to why we ought to stay together, I silently ran through the reasons to justify why we should part. *Grandad would have been disappointed that I was unable to stick it out 'for better or for worse', but I wasn't born in his generation. And anyway, he isn't here any more; and, no, it isn't my ideal to be a single parent, but better that than stuck in a troubled marriage.* Still I felt a crushing sense of guilt and failure, but up ahead, fixed firmly in sight, my two boys bobbed along the dusty Bansko pavements. They didn't know what went on between Sam and me, but they were growing up fast and it wouldn't be long before they saw and heard more than they should. My kids deserved better, all of us did. And so I resolved that the marriage was over.

Ending a relationship is never easy, even when you know it's the right thing to do. But when the emotional strain got too much,

I found time to retreat to the hills. I started to realise, though, that on occasion my lack of experience bordered on the reckless. There was nothing else for it: if I was going to continue to go out on my own, I needed to take the basic course in navigation skills I'd been meaning to do for so long.

The class I attended was held once a week for six weeks at Drumnadrochit, a short drive from Inverness along the A82 towards Fort William, where a bunch of us stumbled around a field with black binbags over our heads – we must've looked crazy. We had to take a bearing on a given landmark, set our compass, then walk on the bearing to reach it. I learnt to work out how many paces I take to cover 100 metres, which for me, by the way, is 66 on average ground, meaning I can travel a distance of about five kilometres an hour. But, more importantly, I learnt enough to be able to go out hillwalking on my own without having to wait for brilliant blue-sky days or to rely on others to do the navigation – because, truthfully, up until now I'd been mostly winging it.

Drumnadrochit also happened to be an access point for Meall Fuar-mhonaidh, the hill that had been a part of the familiar landscape of my childhood. I'd been able to see it from the beach at the end of our garden and from the top of Cromal Mount out front of our house. Of all the mountains in the surrounding landscape it was this one that was most distinctive, shaped like a great big Christmas pudding, missing only a sprig of holly on its top. It was a place where Mum's fiancé Gerry had liked to take her on days out – not up the hill itself, but along Loch Ness – and the area had remained a favourite. Though I was only little, I remember

Gerry would borrow my grandad's orange car to drive Mum and me there, and it was one of these days – just as we motored through Inverness, passing the big whisky distillery on the left with its blackened stone walls and, on the right, huge dirty gas tanks beyond the railway tracks – that Gerry gave me a present. My mum passed it back to me: *A Treasury of Nursery Rhymes*, illustrated by Hilda Boswell. I loved it – it remained one of my most treasured childhood possessions – and I loved him.

So although I knew Meall Fuar-mhonaidh well, and it meant a great deal to me, I'd never actually walked up it. It was a Monday morning of the last week in February 2010 when I finally went to the top. That day, when I looked out of our window, the sky was such a brilliant blue it was as though it had somehow detached itself from above Cyprus or some other Mediterranean land. I checked the local forecast: it was going to remain a settled day in the north-east.

I'd had a thoroughly hideous weekend off the back of an equally rotten week and getting out onto the hillside sounded like exactly what I needed.

'Who'd like to go up the Christmas pudding hill?' I called, rousing the boys from their sleep.

'MEEE!' They cried in unison from behind closed doors, and I laughed.

'Come on then. Let's get ready and we'll go.'

I was glad they wanted to come because it would give us a chance to talk through everything that had been happening. I had to make sure they were okay about Sam not living with us any more.

In their cosy salopettes the boys struck out with me along the footpath next to a small stream. Silver birches overcrowded each bank, their dark branches interlocking above the gurgling flow, and fallen limbs forming natural bridges. The air was crisp and clear, with just a hint of the scent of leaf mould where its russet patches remained exposed next to the water. Soft snow creaked underfoot, and moisture that had dripped from grasses overhanging the stream had frozen into icy chandeliers. Leon was a bright-red streak against the white, as he made straight for the bank to kick snow into the icy river, while Marcus, a mirror of the blue sky above, ambled on ahead.

On our right lay unbroken wide, open space under a thick white blanket, spreading towards the lower shoulder of Meall Fuar-mhonaidh. At closer quarters the hill had lost its prominent dome shape; instead the changed perspective gave it the appearance of a whale surfacing for air. And what I had assumed might be a reasonably steep climb all the way to the top was actually going to be a fairly gradual ascent. Perhaps I needed to try to look at life from a different angle too. Yes, I was upset that I'd finally had to call it a day with Sam, and the break-up had somehow renewed my grief for my mother – she was the one I wanted to be able to turn to through all of this – but my health was good, my children fantastic and we had a roof over our heads. And I *was* grateful for these things, sometimes I just felt too overwhelmed by everything to remember all that we had going for us.

The stream's chanting grew softer as the path curved away and crossed a track through two gates. We walked through woodland of birch and hazel, feeling through the soles of our boots the network of roots bulging like varicose veins under old, papery skin. As we climbed more steeply the trees began to thin out, until all at once we were completely surrounded by wintry moorland. We came upon a stile over deer fencing so big that it was like a climbing frame, and the boys took great pleasure in scaling its grand height to stand on the wooden platform like kings of the castle. They threw snowballs, and one just missed me; on hitting the ground it fractured into tiny pieces that scattered along the ice-encrusted surface.

There wasn't a whisper of wind when I crouched down and picked up a handful of icy crystals. Pouring them slowly through my fingers, I watched and listened as their glittery brilliance chinked and tinkled back onto the sugary terrain. It was mesmerising. On the mountains my senses were honed; light made everything appear brighter and sounds much richer. My mother would have loved this, I knew. I wished we'd come up here together, revisiting one of the places we both associated so much with Gerry. As usual, thinking of her brought an ache to my heart. I pulled my mobile phone from my pocket and wrote her a text – it didn't matter that she could never receive it. I pretended that she would.

When it came to the opposite sex, it seemed I was genetically hardwired to disastrous affairs of the heart – Mum's record had been no better. But of her failed romantic entanglements there was one she had told me to try to learn from.

I was in my teens and I'd just returned home from an adventure holiday in the South of France. I hadn't phoned ahead, as I'd wanted my arrival to be a surprise. Mum wasn't at the flat so I set off on foot to my grandparents' house, anticipating the welcome and the quiz on how I'd got on. Instead I was greeted with the image of my mother lying curled up and shaking on their sofa.

'What's wrong?' I questioned Gran when Mum didn't even look at me.

'She's been like that all weekend,' Gran said. My grandad took me through to the kitchen.

'Your mum was beaten up on Friday.'

'What! Why?'

'All I can tell you is that she arrived here at the back door, her face so covered in blood I didn't recognise her at first. The doctor came out at two in the morning. Stones ingrained into the palms of her hands had to be scrubbed out and then she was taken to Raigmore for X-rays. Her head had been knocked so hard off a wall she was temporarily deafened in one ear. If two men hadn't come out of the pub and stopped it God knows what would have happened.'

The attacker had been Mum's boyfriend, but she didn't press charges. Instead, two months later she succumbed to his apologies and flowers and announced they were seeing each other again. 'It wasn't him, it was the drink,' she said. 'It won't happen again. He's said he'll change.'

Of course, he did not. And he went on to cheat. Mum told me she'd seen them together, walking by the riverside hand in hand. 'Hi, Jen,' he'd said, all casual, like she was nothing special to him. At home, in a fit of rage, she shredded everything he'd ever given her. She took the tattered, broken items and scattered them over his garden. It was the one and only time I'd ever known her to act so wildly. When he tried to win her round again, this time, for her, it was over.

We all have our own threshold of how far we are prepared to go before the game is finally up. People don't change unless they really want to, and, like my mum, I'd had to learn this lesson the hard way too. I'd kept trying with Sam, because he'd kept telling me he loved me, and I wanted to believe that. I found myself stuck in the same sort of relationship as my mother, repeating her mistakes. When it came down to the choice of me or a bottle, I'd never stood much chance, I was almost used to that. But when I discovered a mass of online messages to a string of other women, I should have realised I was never going to be enough.

As I climbed over the stile I lingered briefly to catch a glimpse of the loch, most of it hidden by the intervening slopes. Once we gained the ridge we stayed on its left, the way clearly marked as we followed footprints trodden deep into the snow. Leon wanted to make his own tracks but quickly gave up. 'It's too hard work,' he said as he flumped down, picked up some snow and ate it.

After we passed a knobble of rock there was a slight dip before we began a more direct ascent of the hill, and the last 100 metres were steeper still, but posed no difficulty as old, sunken footprints carved out a snowy staircase. Marcus sprang ahead. I was lost in admiration when, somewhere from behind, a familiar, high-pitched screech like a gull interrupted my thought.

'*Muum!*' Leon squawked, 'my legs are going to fall off. I have to stop.'

'We've really not got far to go, we're almost at the top. Come on, you've done brilliantly well. Keep going!' I said, remembering that I'd moaned over less on walks with my own mum. Tugging at her trouser leg I'd repeatedly asked, 'Are we nearly there yet?' or 'How far now?' or 'When will we be home?' and she'd had to answer with small untruths like 'Not far now,' or 'Just around the next corner' or 'It won't be long.' By my standards, Leon was doing great. Mum would have been proud of him.

I found myself wishing, not for the first time, that my children had had the chance to know her. That she'd had the chance to know them. I'd always talked to them about her. And when they were small they'd at least known the sound of her voice because I'd played them bedtime stories she'd recorded on tapes. That had meant so much to me. But these much-loved treasures were lost to us for ever, all chewed up by the cassette recorder. If she had been here she would have read to them all the time. She would have played games, sung to them while playing her guitar, taken them for walks or to the park – and I would never have had to worry about arranging childcare, she'd have been stealing them off me! She would have looked after them the same way my grandparents had done for her with me. Remembering how much I had benefited from that close and important relationship I'd had with my own grandparents made me regret even more how my boys were missing out.

Reaching a cairn on what appeared to be the summit, we noticed that the true top lay further west. 'I'm staying here. Collect me on the way back,' stated Leon. Marcus and I exchanged a look and agreed to carry on without him, knowing full well he'd soon follow. We dropped down a short distance before we were traipsing up once again to reach a flat plateau. It didn't take much more than five to ten minutes to arrive at the real peak, and as we neared the piled-up stones a fast crunching over snow behind us announced the imminent arrival of the one and only Leon. Spinning round, we cheered, and a gigantic smile spread across his face as I welcomed him into my arms.

It had been warm work reaching the top, though now we'd stopped we cooled rapidly, so we stayed at the summit only long enough to eat rolls, slug freezing water and take in the panoramic scene in silence. In every direction we were surrounded by a glut of gleaming white peaks, row after row rippling off into the distance, pristine, angled outlines against a deep-blue sky. The clean, dry air brought down from Arctic regions made views down the Great Glen to Ben Nevis appear stunningly clear. Snow had transformed the landscape, hiding heathers and grasses, and it was so cold there was not a flying insect to be seen; and yet I felt flooded by the presence of life. We were removed from the chaos and noise that carried on way down beneath us – people buzzing past in cars to-ing and fro-ing from appointments, folk bustling around shops, and workers in offices or on building sites – all oblivious to us up here by ourselves.

'Look,' I said to the boys, pointing, 'you can see Fort George from here.' We'd been to the Fort, and the village where I'd grown up, on our bikes many times. And as much as I had done with my mum, they too loved clambering to the top of Cromal Mount, where we'd look across the smudge of Inverness to the inverted bowl we now stood upon.

As we retraced our steps across the plateau, the race was on between the boys. 'Last one to that lump stinks of tuna!' Marcus yelled. I watched contentedly as they ran. I'd tentatively broached the subject of Sam earlier in the day and they had said they didn't mind that he didn't live with us any more. Listening to their laughter and shrieks escaping into the still air, I was reassured they were indeed all right. And so was I.

The end of my relationship with Sam had marked the beginning of a new and, I hoped, better phase for me. With every mountain I was climbing, I was becoming fitter physically and growing stronger mentally. I'd come to realise since separating that the main reason I'd married Sam was because I'd been afraid to be alone, but it hadn't solved anything. Now I finally understood that being alone could be the more attractive option. My marriage hadn't failed; it had been a mistake from the start. And I hadn't let my children down; they were doing just fine.

And now I was on course for a new, exciting challenge: Kilimanjaro. I felt more resolute than ever that the effort of the journey to its top would help me to put all of my troubles firmly behind me – after all, the name of the mountain's peak itself, Uhuru, meant freedom.

TROUBLED TRACKS

'But helpless Pieces of the Game He plays
Upon this Chequer-board of Nights and Days;
Hither and thither moves, and checks, and slays,
And one by one back in the Closet lays.'

The Rubaiyat *of Omar Khayyam, LXIX*

CHAPTER SEVEN

Keep Them Close

Nakara, Tanzania, June 2010

It was the eve of my flight to Tanzania. Four days earlier I'd been on Braeriach with my children, but now Marcus had been packed off on a school trip to an outdoor-activity centre for a week, and Sam had agreeably upheld his offer to look after Leon. I was on my own at last, sitting on a bed in a hotel room near Edinburgh airport. It was almost liberating in itself to have no responsibilities for the next ten days. After all the changes and upheavals that had been going on, and all the preparation involved for this trip, I finally had the chance to put my foot on the brake for a while.

Clutched in the palm of one hand was a tiny pot containing some of Mum's ashes. I knew she would have loved to return to East Africa, so a piece of her was coming with me. In my other hand was a photograph of the two of us, taken at the top of Cromal Mount, the Fort in the background. As I looked at the image of our smiling faces, feeling the familiar sadness swelling, I thought about the imminent ascent of Kilimanjaro: I knew it was going to be tough, but I had to succeed. It was as though the two things were tied – the grief that I hadn't been able to shake had driven me to take on this challenge, and if anything was going to get me to the top it would be holding tightly to thoughts of Mum, a determination to keep going in her memory. A part of me was also excited to think that I'd be, in a way, following in Gerry's footprints, becoming a big mountain climber.

Lying in the hotel bed too excited to sleep, I fantasised that I'd made it to the mountain's peak and was overlooking Kenyan plains, towards the places of my mother's childhood. In 1960 my grandad had been posted to a place called Lanet, six miles from the town of Nakuru, about 100 miles from Nairobi. The family lived on a military base, and home was a large, red-roofed bungalow with a huge garden. Mum was about eight years old then. I imagined her as a little girl, all prim and proper in her purple and white gingham dress, ready for the journey to school in Nakuru. There was no bus for the dozen or so kids from the army base who attended Lugard, so instead they were transported to school on the back of a one-ton army truck. Five minutes before it was due to leave, a hand-cranked air-raid siren would sound and Mum, along with all the other kids, would belt down the road.

I'd heard the stories so many times when I was younger and had always found them fascinating. It sounded so exciting – so different from my own childhood experiences. Still, growing up in a military background, Mum had had a fairly rigid upbringing, I knew. I wondered if that's what had made her so wild and free-spirited during her teenage years. Still not asleep in the darkening airport hotel room, I thought back to my own childhood and the experiences that had played their part in defining the person I became.

I was five, living with my grandparents, and had just started school. My mother was in Aberdeen and had begun a second year of teacher training. I would only see her on holidays, and her commitment to the four-year course was already taking its toll on my long-term, and already fragile, security. I was quite reserved. Going to school was the first time I'd mixed with local children, and this only made me more timid – I may as well have walked into that playground with a big placard emblazoned with the words 'easy target'.

Set back from the road and surrounded by farmland, the old stone school building was situated two miles outside the village, and it was there that a girl, a couple of years my senior, made it her business to terrorise me. Bullying didn't happen every day, but its impact over the course of two years stayed with me. Playtime and home time had always been the worst. Deliberately seeking me out, the robust, red-cheeked girl would order me to the end of the playing field, where she'd humiliate me by pulling up my skirt, teasing that she was going to pull down my pants and tickle me or 'get me' after school; but what hurt a million times more than her threats was when she would tell me that my mother didn't love or care about me. On and on she would taunt.

My grandad and her mother would take turns to do the school run home. I dreaded the ride home with her – sitting next to me on the back seat, she would deliberately squash me against the door, pinch my legs hard and sneakily tug my hair. And then one day I was invited to her home. I'd thought she wanted to be my friend now. We played in some woods out of sight from her house, where I picked up a colourful plastic ball. 'That had poison on it. You'll be dead by tomorrow,' she jeered. She made me follow her to a wooden fence where we sat on top of its stile.

'Kiss me,' she ordered.

'Where?' I asked, feeling hugely afraid of her answer.

'On my mouth,' she said, with unflinching coldness. I obeyed.

After that the prospect of having to go to school made me feel sick. I'd complain to my grandparents that I didn't want to go, that I didn't like it, but I was too frightened to reveal the truth.

When my mum came home on holiday I was her shadow. She'd take me on walks along the beach where broom crackled in the summer heat and sweet coconut-scented gorse grew so wildly, its smell mingling with the salty seaside air. She taught me the difference between these similar species, pointed out dog rose and other wild flowers and plants, or birds like the yellowhammers that flew between the thickets and seabirds like the oystercatchers and curlews. We'd have picnics on white sands round the back of the Fort and play at running away from the waves. We'd search for razor clams, perfectly intact whelks and stamp on the seaweed to hear it pop. And at home she'd play songs to me on her guitar. All of these things were reassurance that the bully was wrong and that I was loved, but time always passed too quickly and Mum would leave once more for Aberdeen.

Separation was upsetting; I didn't want her to go because her departure also spelt back to school and into the clutches of my tormentor. Eventually I was moved to the village school, but the damage was already done and I was shy and awkward around the other kids for the rest of my school years, distrusting people's motives while also being convinced I was unlikeable. I spent a fairly solitary and lonely childhood, deriving happiness from the company of the adults at home and by losing myself in drawing and painting – mainly on the walls, which did not go down a storm with Gran.

Later, during my teen years, my grandad would sometimes ask why I was either up or down and never a happy medium. I used to tell him it was because of my inherent artistic temperament, and while I decided there probably was some truth in that, I also believed I'd been conditioned by those early experiences: swinging between the extremes of feeling great joy when Mum was home from college, to deep term-time doom. Where my mother had spent her teens rebelling against her parents in pursuit of independence, I had wanted to stay as close to her as possible.

It was an early start the next day, but it felt full of promise. And after an eight-hour flight the aircraft began its descent to Dar es Salaam, Tanzania. As we reached a height of 5,000 metres, I realised that in a few days my feet – like those belonging to the other 35,000 people who also come to climb this mountain each year – would be trekking higher than this. It seemed both fantastic and implausible.

After immigration and baggage reclaim I exited the airport and found my way to other waiting members of the Marie Curie fundraising team. I'd been to Africa before, visiting Malawi and Egypt, but the wall of heat and the monstrously proportioned bugs still came as a surprise. The driver launched our rucksacks and holdalls onto the roof of our transport, a minibus that looked like the Mystery Machine from *Scooby-Doo*, and funnily enough our short and stocky, bespectacled trek doctor, Emma, with her auburn fringed bob, bore more than a passing resemblance to Velma. There weren't enough seats in the bus for everyone, so I travelled to the hotel by Jeep with Marty – who would also be my roomie during the trip. Marty and I came from the same town and we knew each other a little, so it was nice to have a familiar face to share a hotel room and tent with.

We set off and almost immediately petrol fumes and the stench of rotting animal flesh rushed in through the open windows, filling my nostrils and making me feel very ill. But as the countryside opened up, these odours were replaced by the smells of burning bush from local farms. For two hours the bumpy ride continued until finally we arrived at Nakara Hotel, which, at an elevation of around 1,500 metres, was higher than Ben Nevis. The queasiness passed and the intoxicating and heady scent of jasmine permeated the night air. Above us a sumptuous, deep-velvet sky was punctuated by a scattering of stars. I already felt better.

Last down for breakfast, I was dismayed to find that everything was pretty much gone, so I had a juice then took a short walk before our briefing. I'd read up on high-altitude trekking and was aware of the risks involved; these were made more stark by our medic, Emma. 'The higher you go the more important it is to drink plenty of fluids. Dehydration is dangerous on its own, but it can also mask or worsen altitude sickness. If your pee is dark, you aren't drinking enough. Your headache could lead to cerebral oedema and coughs may be the precursor to pulmonary oedema. Both are life-threatening and in either event we need to get you down off the mountain quickly.'

Later, all twenty-five of us set out for an acclimatisation walk around the local area along the soft, reddish-brown soil road which, because of the rain, seemed to have turned into a kind of wet clay. Streets were simply openings in thick plantations of maize or banana trees. Winding paths the width of a foot supported the occasional kiosk, whose goods were random and sparse – three of this, four of that. Soaps and washing powder sold alongside half a dozen tomatoes and an avocado, all ensconced behind a wire mesh to stop thieves. I bought a piece of sugar cane from a young boy for a dollar. Its stick-like shape and fibrous texture reminded me of the rhubarb Grandad once grew in his garden, but my taste buds felt robbed because it wasn't the sugary treat I'd expected. We walked on through luscious green foliage above a rock-strewn river, and beyond its bank was a field being worked by women, breaking the soil with antiquated scythes. It looked an arduous task under the blaze of the afternoon sun, but on seeing us they raised their hands to wave and flashed a smile.

Musky wood and a fresh, earthy scent from overnight rain filled the air as we passed by ramshackle homes, tucked in behind the trees, almost completely hidden from sight. At the Marangu Gate, where our trek would end, Humphrey, our local guide, pointed out the Chyulu Hills to the north and Lake Chala to the south-east, the Kenyan border tucked in behind.

As our trekking group walked along winding paths I saw what I assumed was a shallow grave. The low bed of rocks was fringed with grasses that had since dried out, some plants grew in between and at its head was a colourful wreath and a crude wooden cross. When I asked, Humphrey confirmed my thoughts. The family had buried their loved one close by. I could understand why they would want to do that. I held tightly on to the tiny pot of Mum's ashes in my pocket.

CHAPTER EIGHT

Where the Wind Blows

Naro Moru Gate to Simba Camp, 2,650 metres/
Simba Camp to Kikelewa, 3,678 metres, June 2010

O ur group's Land Cruisers left the hotel early and headed in a northerly direction to bring us around Mount Kilimanjaro to Rongai and the Naro Moru Gate at an elevation of 1,950 metres. It was a bone-shaking ride, but the scenery provided distraction. A car passed, toiling on the slight incline, and my eyes almost popped out of their sockets as I took in the vision of this clapped-out hunk of rust bursting at its seams. It was jammed full of bodies, five people crammed into the front and seven or eight in the rear. I felt claustrophobic just looking at them.

Women wearing vibrant fabrics and carrying impossibly huge cargoes of bananas on their heads were in colourful contrast to the dry and dusty landscape, and a man in a checked shirt and dirty, rag-hemmed trousers laboured uphill on his bike loaded with blue-plastic gallon containers full of water. There were market stalls at the roadside of each small township we passed through, where men sat under shade on rickety wooden stools chatting over a drink, and women stood at the road with baskets of beef tomatoes and sacks of maize to sell.

On arrival at the Gate we were given cucumber sandwiches and tea. Fellow trekkers got to know each other better as they chatted inside the simple concrete gazebo, but I shied away. Fuelled by my fear of rejection, a wave of regret for having come as part of a large group flowed through me; feeling uncomfortable, I wandered off and watched with interest as a straggly queue of around forty porters waited to have loads weighed. Seeing Humphrey, I asked how the expedition was organised. 'Well, the team has six guides, and they carry their own kit, nothing else. The tent boys carry the tents, set them up and clean them out each day. The three cooks have to carry only the eggs, but once the eggs run out they have to help carry other stuff. And the porters have to carry the clients' kit, their own and whatever else is required,' he said. It didn't seem possible that these short, wiry men would carry so much.

Before we began the trek proper I thought I'd better go for a posh pee (by this I mean enjoyment of a pee in the comfort of a facility with a flushing loo, a basin to wash in, warm water and maybe a paper towel to dry my hands), but what I was directed to was something far removed from my expectations: as surprising as the porters' loads was my first encounter with the long-drop. Several metres from the gazebo was a shaky wooden structure; inside the cubicle was a rectangular opening cut into its slatted floor from which a powerful stench was emanating from the pit underneath. I gagged but managed to urinate, and I reckon it was at this point that my bowels beat an immediate retreat into hibernation. I wondered if I would survive for ten whole days without doing a poo and shuddered as I imagined the headaches and malaise I'd suffer as a consequence of my body absorbing its own toxins. There was no two shades of shit about it, the long-drops were a stinky, messy and off-putting affair, but better them than nothing at all.

Gulping at the fresh air I practically fell out of the wooden cubicle, straightened myself up and rejoined the group, which was getting organised to begin the trek. At the entrance to the Kilimanjaro National Park was a warning sign that quickly replaced any toileting fears I'd had. A series of blackened planks nailed across two wooden posts and engraved with instructions alerted trekkers on Points to Remember (nine in all) when climbing to high altitude; they all seemed to indicate that what we were about to do was pretty risky. But the unease those rules stirred in me also melted away as we journeyed up through lush tropical rainforest and fields of maize to the chorus of cicadas.

Always preferring my own company when walking, I trailed behind the group till they were out of sight and their chatter was replaced by the sound of my feet scuffing the ground; only Humphrey walked behind me. We'd already passed slender firs with pale-green needles, a delicate relative of the more coarse Scots pines that were so familiar to me. But it was amid the olive, juniper and tall, twisting cedar trees that the rustling of leaves alerted us to a small troop of piebald colobus monkeys who peered down from branches in curiosity.

Somewhere I could hear the soft sound of grasses being trampled and a tapping noise. It grew louder and, turning to locate its source, I spotted a little boy. He appeared through tall green shoots of maize chasing after a large, plastic blue lid that he thwacked merrily with his stick. This happy little lad, who had emerged from the nearby collection of pitiful-looking huts with his makeshift toy, rushed on without giving me a second glance. I thought of my own children and wished they could be here with me. I wanted them to see how much pleasure could be derived from such simple things as a lid and a stick, but mostly I wanted them here because I realised how much I missed them.

At our first camp, clouds drifted apart fleetingly to give teasing views of one of Kilimanjaro's three main volcanic cones. Mawenzi's dark mass was impressive, its brittle, jagged ridge like a thorny crown. The moment of awe was disrupted by loud banter, the other members of the group chatting excitedly about their adventure. I felt apart from their noise and jovialities; I was here to resolve my inner turmoil. But while I was craving some solitude, I also knew that deep down I really did also want to join in with them. At once I felt both resentful and envious of these people with their carefree, light-hearted ways. Feeling my frustration and anger arising within, I wanted to scream at the world from the top of my lungs.

'Hot water?' A voice called from the outside the tent the next morning.

'Yeah, *asante*,' I mumbled.

'*Hakuna matata*.'

Six o'clock awakenings and that minimal exchange of conversation would become the norm for the duration of our time on the mountain. My roomie Marty and I stirred to wakefulness by using the small Tupperware bowls of water we'd each been provided with to clean ourselves. It wasn't a big deal to either of us that we didn't know each other that well. We accepted the situation for what it was, which was a good job, because turning our backs on each other to wash then dress was all the privacy we were going to get. After packing our gear we headed to the canteen tent, where breakfast consisted of a hard-boiled egg, whose yolk appeared more white than yellow, and a radioactive bright-pink sausage; we looked dubiously at our plates.

It was the second day of the trek and we were walking to camp two, Kikelewa – a significant height gain of 1,028 metres. On the way, while others conversed about farts, their lack of bowel movements, and the celebrities who had climbed Kilimanjaro for the Comic Relief charity months earlier, I fretted about altitude sickness.

'*Pole, pole,*' Humphrey said.

'What's that mean?' I asked.

'Slowly, slowly. You'll acclimatise better.'

So I stayed at the back of our group and maintained a deliberately slow pace, thinking Humphrey's advice was an iron-clad guarantee against mountain sickness; and he kept me company.

'What's that plant? . . . What do you call this? . . . What do you call that?' On and on I went.

'The buds of this plant are special; this variety is collected and infused in water then used to swill around the mouth to ease dental pain. It has antiseptic properties,' he said. 'There are many plants and trees that have medicinal value. This one helps stomach upsets, we use the aerial root of the tree and boil it, then when it cools it is drunk,' Humphrey said, touching the bark of a fig tree. Flat clumps of everlastings spread in abundance; their white petals with yellow centres reminded me of daisies.

'What are these?' I asked, pointing at seven pretty red flowers supported on a wiry stem, their heads closed because of heavy moisture in the air.

'They are gladiolus, named after one of the first Westerners to climb this mountain. From now on plants will become less,' Humphrey answered.

'What's the name of that bird with the pale streaks on its face?'

'It's a streaky seedeater. Its home is on the moorland.'

Asking about the birds and plants was just one of my ways to remember Mum out loud, and with great patience Humphrey did his best to answer the barrage of questions. I was feeling good; both my body and my mind were invigorated by the exercise and stimulated by the unfamiliar.

Trees and larger plants began to diminish as we plodded higher. We'd been on the move for about four hours through damp mists with no views, but by midday the full force of the sun blazed overhead. I stopped for a drink and, on turning round to take in the scenery, I was bewitched by the most incredible sight. Tropical clouds were a thick and fluffy sea of white colliding silently into the side of the mountain, the sky above a perfect deep blue. I felt as if I were in a secret land in the sky and had to point out the phenomenon to Marty.

'Oh aye, cloud inversion. You sometimes see that on the mountains at home. Pretty cool, isn't it?' he said, and carried on walking. But his matter-of-factness didn't trash my sense of awe; it *was* really cool, and I tried to walk backwards for a bit to enjoy it for longer.

When we stopped to break, after stashing my daysack in the canteen tent's shade, I found a spot where I could sit and admire the ocean of white. Nearby, a white-naped raven strutted about on top of Third Cave – a large lava tube – no doubt waiting expectantly for the leftovers from our lunch.

After eating we rested another half-hour, giving the porters time to dismantle the tent, wash up pots and dishes and filter water from the river to refill our bottles. It made me feel guilty that they were doing all the work while all we had to do was eat the food we were given and walk. I took a short stretch to Third Cave and sat away from everyone until it was time to resume the trek. I watched the raven, still on its own, still keenly waiting for us to move on so that it could scavenge for scraps. It made me think about the elusive heron that Mum and I had liked to catch a glimpse of on the river at home.

Back on the trail I walked alone until an older fellow trekker, Robby, joined me. I hadn't been desirous of company but he was Liverpudlian, and that reminded me of Gran. I asked if he was familiar with Bootle – the town where Gran had grown up, had met my grandad, and where Mum had been born. He was. And, having found an admittedly tenuous link to my family's history, I allowed myself to relax with him a little. It was as we were walking and playing our made-up game, 'Name That Hum', that we began to notice the effects of altitude and the game didn't last long because trying to think up trivia was too tasking.

It seemed the rest of the group was experiencing it too; we soon caught up with three of the younger women from our group, none of them feeling well. Two of them had suffered terrible diarrhoea during the night and were now feeling nauseous and had headaches. It surprised me that people were becoming ill so soon into the trek. Robby and I walked on in a serious silence until, unexpectedly, the most giant fart erupted from his ass, but when I then let one rip too we both fell about the mountainside laughing.

After stopping for a short break in the afternoon, Marty joined Robby and me to walk at the rear.

'What *are* you doing?' I asked Marty, as I turned round to see him standing stock-still and pushing at his belly.

'I'm trying to make all my farts come out at once . . .' he strained. 'That's why I came to the back,' he gasped, his face reddening with the exertion. All three of us started howling with laughter. The wind, jokes and giggles, almost to the point of hysteria, all continued until we reached our evening campsite; we blamed it on the altitude.

After an eight-hour trek, the ritual unpacking and dinner, the day ended with a hot chocolate under the night sky. To the north the sky was comparatively empty, but southwards a plethora of stars were splattered on a black-canvas sky like a Jackson Pollock painting, stunning, bright and clear. As I gazed up at those other worlds I reflected on the day: it had been better, thanks to Robby and Marty. I'd take each day as I found it. *Yeah, go with the wind!* the voice in my head giggled. *Enjoy the hill. 'Cause if your mum was here she'd be loving all this!*

CHAPTER NINE

Where There's a Will
There's a Way

Kikelewa to Mawenzi Tarn, 4,295 metres/
Mawenzi to Kibo, 4,700 metres, June 2010

M arty woke me around three in the morning when he got up for a pee. A pounding headache that had settled in earlier now burned behind my right eye. I'd also managed to get a lump of beef stuck between my teeth at dinner which I hadn't been able to dislodge when I'd brushed, and now the gum around my tooth throbbed away uncomfortably. Toothache was no fun under normal circumstances, let alone up a remote mountain miles from help. But I'd have been more worried about it if I didn't already know that dental issues at altitude were not unusual, even fillings can shrink. And, anyway, it was far from my only concern. The number of people with mild symptoms of acute mountain sickness (AMS) had risen from three to five in one day, and I was afraid that I might become the sixth. During the remaining hours of the night, sleep was fractured as exhaustion battled against my aches and paranoia. Those hours had been rough, but by light my tooth had settled and, after giving myself a thorough wash, I put on some clean clothes and felt fresher. Even breakfast was enjoyable, and after some quick stretching exercises our group worked its way up into the Highland Desert Zone.

Everlastings carpeted the ground between clumps of stubby yellow grasses in shades of patchy greens and browns like dried tobacco. The winding trail ascended gradually until even the green began to disappear and lava tubes, like giant wormholes, became the focus of interest. Behind lay the ocean of cloud, but up ahead the dark outline of Mawenzi's broken ridge punctured the skyline, like an African version of Skye's rocky Cuillin range. Up ahead was the site of our next camp.

It had taken four hours, but we arrived over a knoll and dropped down into a hollow bowl during early afternoon. Mawenzi Tarn lay still, its shrunken egg shape framed by a halo of iridescent green algae. It looked toxic, but I was told it was going to be the source of our water supply. Nice. As we neared the tents we were welcomed with an amazing reception from our porters, a merry ragbag band dressed in bright pinks and blues, one trouser leg up one trouser leg down. Arms raised and swaying like a gospel choir, they danced and sang their Kilimanjaro song in joyous harmony. Singing to us, singing to the mountain – hoping it would bless us and keep us all safe from harm and the dangers of high altitude.

It was after lunch, when we were briefed on the next morn-ing's itinerary, that I felt a rush of anticipation. Summit night, the climax of our trip, was a day closer than I'd realised. It was time to exorcise my demons. This was what I'd come for . . .

An afternoon's acclimatisation walk on to Mawenzi took us up another couple of hundred metres onto its east ridge over scree and dark rock. Akin to Cuillin gabbro, it felt like Velcro underfoot and was great to scramble over. Sitting on the ridge under the sun's glare I kept to myself; a dull ache at the back of my head was making me feel more unsociable than usual. As I looked down into the bowl, beneath sweeping volcanic slopes, our tents appeared like bright flecks of orange punctuation on a dark and grainy page. We were higher than anyone in the world below could see, even higher than the clouds. Absorbed in the rugged beauty, it was a while before I noticed that my headache had begun to shift, but when I did my mood instantly buoyed and remained that way when we got back down to camp.

As the sun lowered on the horizon the temperature dropped sharply, so I layered up and, with half an hour to spare before dinner, I took myself off over the rocky outcrop behind our tent. Finding a flattish ledge on a finger between two gullies, I sat down to soak in the view. Gentle hues in pastel shades of pink merged softly with yellows and tangerine. Higher above, cornflower blue deepened into indigo and I marvelled at all the wonder of this colour, concealed by cauliflower clouds from life beneath. A waxing moon hung low in the sky, and under my watchful stare it sunk lower still. In the peaceful twilight, I was alone with my memories.

Though Mum's brain tumour had been removed, the disease had rampaged through her and its symptoms presented themselves too quickly. It was August 1997, seven weeks before she died. We sat with a brandy each and we talked. I'd had the idea of asking her to tape some stories and nursery rhymes – the tapes that ended up meaning so much to both me and my sons – but I hadn't found the right time to bring it up. Her persistent cough was getting worse, so I knew I had to ask soon, but it was only after a little Dutch courage that I was able to broach it.

'What do you want me to do that for?'

'So that if I ever have a child I can play the tape to them, so that they'll know who their grandma is.' I hadn't wanted to upset her, but she smiled back at me.

'I think that's a lovely idea!'

'Awesome! We can get tapes on the weekend,' I said, as my mother suddenly made a sharp intake of breath and her face creased. 'What's wrong? Where do you hurt?'

'It's my back this time,' she groaned. Touching her gently, I willed her not to hurt – and the discomfort eased.

'Imagine if I really did have healing hands?' I said. 'I just want to fix you.'

'You have in a way,' she replied. I still don't know what she meant by that, but, the pain having passed, at the time it didn't feel right to press her.

Early the following morning Mum's coughing woke me. I walked into the living room to check that she was all right. She was sitting on the sofa, wrapped in her purple dressing gown, staring fixedly at the television.

'It makes you want to cry,' she said, not shifting her gaze.

I looked at the flickering images being broadcast. News was being reported live that Princess Diana had died at four in the morning following a traffic accident in Paris.

'Life is a lottery,' Mum added sadly.

I turned my attention back to her as she wiped the end of her nose with a tissue, and I wondered if she was also thinking of herself.

I'd been worried about Marty during the night: his breathing was terrible, he'd been coughing and was restless. I hadn't thought it was the best idea to smoke a big reefer every night before crashing out (scoring some grass from a local had been first on his to-do list on arrival at our hotel), and it sounded as though I was right. Complaining about a headache, he had gone to find the medic, and I fell back into broken sleep till he returned.

'What did Emma say?' I asked.

'She gave me Diamox.' His perfunctory response made me realise just how much he was suffering – ordinarily Marty could talk the hind legs off not just one but a whole herd of donkeys.

'Hope it works for you,' I said in sympathy. But, unless his taking it had the placebo effect, I had my doubts. While the drug is an aid to acclimatisation, there's no guarantee that it will either prevent or relieve symptoms of AMS. My own doctor had told me it wasn't necessary to take it, but that if I did want to use it, it would be best to begin taking the pills a few days before I started climbing, so the drug was already at work in the system. I chose not to take it.

'It's fucking freezing, I'm putting more layers on.' Now I was wearing two pairs of thick socks, a T-shirt, fleece, windstopper and both my down jackets.

Marty coughed. 'I feel like shit,' he said. And with that we settled down as best we could. Both of us woke often. As I tossed and turned like a giant blue caterpillar on my sleeping mat I was conscious of my breathing and the need to inhale deeply.

In the morning it was Marty's coughing that stirred me to full wakefulness. As we ventured out only the porters were about, beginning the daily water-boiling ritual and preparing the canteen for breakfast. I returned to my slab on the finger of rock to watch the sunrise; it was as evocative as the previous evening's sunset. Orange beams of warm light stretched forward in a burst of rays and heat to greet the new day, dispelling the night's discomfort. And I basked in its glow.

A few weeks after Mum had made the tapes of nursery rhymes and stories her health deteriorated and I had a bad feeling about what was coming. It was afternoon and she was resting in my bed. I wanted to lie next to her and hold her, but dared not. The last time I had brushed my awkwardness aside to embrace her gently I had hurt her; cancer now made every bit of her ache. So I sat on the carpet with my back against the wall and hugged my knees, drawing them into my chest. The sun's rays filtered through the flimsy yellow gingham curtains, its golden light in harmony with the walls.

'I love this room. I like how the sun makes it feel warm,' she said, as she turned her face towards mine. 'Do you know what I regret? I regret that I'll miss what happens to everyone. And I had looked forward to being a granny.' Once more her words made my heart ache and quite suddenly I felt terrified that time would make me forget how she sounded, looked and smelt.

'I regret I can't give you half my years,' I choked, as anxiety, that now familiar stabbing pain, seared across my chest. I felt hopeless and guilty – guilty for living, and for grieving even though she was still with me. I felt robbed of our future, of laughing, moaning and arguing with her – and that child's voice inside whined. *It's not fair!* The child was screaming and stamping its feet with all its fury and might.

'The only thing I'm worried about is that I'm not going to be around to keep an eye on your spending; it's a bad habit of yours when you're upset.' She paused. 'I wish I could have left you everything, Sarah, but I've written a will.' And then followed another short silence before Mum continued, 'You're the best thing I have ever done; you are my daughter and you're carrying my genes. You have been reliable and true. And you've been here for me in every practical way.' I wished I could carry on doing everything for her for longer, for ever.

'What will I do with you . . . when you are gone . . . what shall I do with your ashes?'

'I won't care, I'll be dead. You do what you think is right. It might take you a while, but you'll get there in the end . . . you always do,' then, not for the first time, she added, 'Just promise me you won't give up.'

'I promise,' I said, trying to sound believable as I swallowed my sadness in the happy glow of the room.

As I left the slab of rock and walked back to camp, the glaciers on Kibo, Kilimanjaro's highest peak, glittered and sparkled as they reflected the light.

At breakfast it was clear that the majority of our group was experiencing the effects of altitude. And on everyone's mind was the prospect of not being allowed to reach the summit, but subdued chatter of hopes and fears closed when we were briefed by our guide, Don.

'Today we are trekking over the Saddle to camp four at Kibo. We'll eat lunch, rest, eat dinner at about five, then I want you all to get some rest or sleep if you can. At eleven o'clock tonight everyone needs to be up and ready to make our summit bid. This is the toughest part of the trek, guys. Dig deep.'

I had been anticipating that promise of hardship and struggle – and the five-hour trek across the alpine desert didn't disappoint. Although cool winds blustered across the barren landscape, the sun's fierce rays burned down, and there was no shelter. The sweltering heat and thirst occupied my thoughts till I saw something curious gleaming in the near distance. I asked our local guide Peter what it was.

'Two years ago a small airplane carrying Italians crashed into Mawenzi. The debris went everywhere,' he said. 'Everything from the wreckage, apart from the four dead bodies, was left on the mountain.' As I approached the fuselage of the plane I saw that it was its white carcass reflecting in the sun that had dazzled my eyes. Cutesy paw prints painted on its empty shell only exaggerated the sense of eeriness.

A long time on the Saddle had passed and I desperately needed to pee. This necessary and basic human function dominated my thoughts as I scoured for some place suitable to drop my pants: a lava bomb, situated some distance off the trail, was going to have to do. By the time I'd sorted myself out, Peter was quite far ahead. As I made tracks towards the guide a perfectly round puff of cloud was tumbling like a massive white beach ball across the high, sandy plain. It was a brilliant photo opportunity, but Peter had my camera so I ran to catch up with him. This was a big mistake. Huge. Almost immediately my lungs felt compressed and tight, as though they were being squeezed. I felt like I was suffocating as I struggled to breathe. Every intake of air was piercing, and by the time I caught up with Peter I genuinely thought I was going to die.

'*Haraka haraka haina baraka!*' Peter said, shaking his head.

'What's . . . that . . . mean?' I said between gulps.

'It means, hurry hurry has no blessings. Up here you have to take it slowly, *pole pole*.'

I'd never experienced pain like it and continued the journey with my head bowed. It occurred to me that I might have destroyed my chance of going to the summit. I had to keep walking and willed myself to take one slow step after the next. Internally I revelled in my rage as the cumulative effects of sun, altitude, hunger, lack of sleep and excruciating chest pain made the going truly hard.

At 4,700 metres Kibo was at an elevation equivalent to Mont Blanc, and I had never been so pleased to reach a camp. In the relative privacy of our tent I was glad for some respite and, once I'd recovered sufficiently, I sorted out kit for the summit attempt. At lunch, word had got round that I'd been unwell and a couple of the trekkers were kind. One lad gave me the last of his concentrated blackcurrant juice, another lent me four AA batteries for my camera and our medic pushed two paracetamol and two Diamox on me. I was glad for the juice and batteries, but there seemed no point in taking the pills now, since I'd almost recovered from my high-altitude sprint. And in any case, I kind of wanted – needed – to feel suffering, as if doing so brought me closer to Mum.

Wednesday, 15 October 1997, was the third-last day of my mother's life. She was in a bad way. Thrush had developed in her throat, and the front of her head was hurting, but she hadn't complained. Her skeletal frame, like that of a woman twice her forty-four years, stumbled into the living room, and her shrunken body was consumed by the brown armchair she sat down into.

'Do you want me to call the doctor?' I asked tentatively.

'Yes,' she said.

Never before had I felt the enormous weight and power of that single word; it terrified me, and in my guts I knew she was near the end. When he came to the flat the doctor wanted to give her morphine for the short journey to hospital, but Mum said no.

'I want to know exactly what's going on. I want to be fully aware,' she answered firmly.

From the front door of the flat my eyes locked onto the two ambulance staff as they lifted my mother, in a chair, down the stairs. One of them grumbled loudly, struggling with the awkwardness of the task. I kept my mouth shut, but inside I was screaming expletives. After calling my grandparents and Frank, I made my own way to the hospital, but on arrival I was sent away almost immediately by my mum.

'Can you go home and fetch me the bangle that Gerry gave me. Don't tell Frank though.'

'Yeah, course I will.' I said unquestioningly. She obviously didn't want to hurt Frank's feelings, and neither did I. When I returned she put it on. I had no doubt she loved Frank, but he was going to carry on living and make a new life for himself eventually. Maybe she knew herself the end was near and perhaps having the bangle gave her some kind of superstitious comfort.

Everyone at camp had taken Don's advice and rested up until we were called for the evening meal, by which time I had recovered from my lung-crushing episode. After eating, a final brief was given.

'Use bottles for your water instead of the CamelBak hydration packs as the tubes are likely to freeze, and I don't want anyone listening to music as we summit. I need your full attention. If another member of the group gets into difficulty you need to be alert and ready to help. I won't lie, this last push is going to hurt. It should take us six hours to get to Gilman's Point and from there it'll take another hour and a half to get around the crater's rim to Uhuru Peak. Some of you won't make it. Altitude sickness can come on rapidly and if you are suffering you must let us know. It will only worsen the higher you go and you will put yourself at serious risk if you continue. There is no point giving everything to get to the summit to realise you can't make it down. Trust me, if you are suffering the only thing you will be thinking is *Get me off this fucking mountain*.'

'I will be joining you all on the ascent until the first person gets sick, and it's not a case of if, but when, because somebody will,' Emma added.

I sat on my camp chair in our canvas canteen and glanced around the faces listening intently, trying to hazard a guess at who might succumb first, hoping upon hope that it wouldn't be me. It was just another lottery.

CHAPTER TEN

Hell on Earth

Kibo to Uhuru Peak,
5,895 metres, June 2010

It was midnight. With no moon I was enfolded by pitch-blackness as I scrambled from the tent. Assembling under the stars, our group came together, headtorches flickering into life. Galvanised into action by Daniel, our summit guide, we set off, slowly and steadily. Marty and I followed in single file directly behind him. My reasons for being up front were purely selfish; we'd been told that if we didn't reach Gilman's Point by 8 a.m. we would not be allowed to continue on to Uhuru Peak – the mountain's true summit. If I was further behind there would be someone slow holding things up. Adrenalin pumped as I felt consumed by a sense of purpose.

The black night was bitterly cold as we trod in small steps on and up. Repetitive monotony of pace, coupled with the intense light powering from my headtorch, made me feel dizzy, but the voice inside my head chattered away again, and before I knew it a whole hour had slipped by.

We continued to snake our way up the scree slope in silence, an occasional mad cry from the guides keeping us amused. We'd been on the move for three hours, climbing 500 vertical metres; and now, as high as Everest Base Camp, we stopped to rest at the cave marking the halfway point to Gilman's. Kitchen porters greeted us with a mug of soup to keep up our fluid intake – and warm us up; I was in awe of their organisation and also very grateful. Murmuring voices clustered together in the darkness, growing in volume as more of our group arrived; their talk, centred on the ascent, flew around in an atmosphere of nervous anticipation while I stood near Daniel wanting to get going. My head throbbed.

As we pressed on into the night the tediousness of the increasingly steep trail felt interminable. I felt light-headed, but the light beaming from my headtorch was also making me feel nauseous, so to distract myself from these unpleasant sensations I began to count from one to a hundred over and over, and over again. Absorbed by this monotonous pastime, I was surprised to suddenly notice we'd reached Gilman's Point. From my high stance, as I looked down the mountainside, the split between groups was more evident: clusters of white light shining from headtorches were separated by some large and some small spans of darkness. Just then Daniel's radio crackled into life.

'I need help with a casualty, and I'm not sure if I'm on the right path back to Kibo. Can you send a guide down?'

'Yeah, okay, Emma,' I heard Don reply over the airwaves. 'Two trekkers were turned round at the Cave. Peter's with them. Stay where you are and he'll look for you as he makes his way down.' I wondered momentarily who was sick, glad it wasn't me.

Trekkers hugged and congratulated each other for making it up to the 5,681m signpost, but we still had 200 vertical metres to gain before we'd reach the true summit. Just before we set off for Uhuru Peak, Marty and I fell out.

'My CamelBak pipe is frozen,' he said.

'I don't mind sharing my water, but I've only got a litre left so we need to take little sips,' I said to him.

'Don't fuckin' bother then,' he answered crankily.

'Marty! We've got at least two hours' walking to get to the top, and then we're gonna have to get all the way back down to camp. All I'm saying is we've got to be sparing.' But Marty stropped off.

It almost felt like being granted the gift of sight when dawn broke and revealed the mountain's features once more. We had transcended those dark hours and trekked into a brand-new colourful day. Optimistically, it felt symbolic. There wasn't so much as a whisper of wind. Cloud, like a herd of white horses galloping noiselessly into the mountain, was again cutting us off from the world below. Ahead, the route along the rim of the crater followed over loose and rocky terrain, dropping down over 100 metres. At the bottom of the steep scree slope on my right was a new view – the dormant volcano's resurgent dome. Straining my eyes, I could just make out a meandering, broken thread of ant-sized people crossing the vast, dusty-brown plain below; in my confused state, their presence was surprising. It was worth a photo, but Don, who seemed to have crept up behind, urged me to hurry on. 'You need to put the camera away. There's no time for hanging about,' he muttered bad-temperedly.

Our original group of twenty-five had become twelve as we walked in a straggling single line, each of us quiet. By now my head was incredibly sore: my eyeballs seemed to be vibrating in their sockets and my face felt hot. My balance was all to fuck, and as I came down off a rock it felt like I'd stepped out on a dead leg, my knees buckling. I knew I was feeling the effects of the altitude but I was determined to keep on going. I'd come so far, giving up was not an option.

Concentrating on breathing, I staggered forward. Movement felt like trying to push through some kind of invisible force field. I felt diabolical . . . hammered and hungover all at once. My hand scraped off a tower of brittle wall on my left. Beyond the Reusch Crater on my right was the ash pit; my vision made the scenes blur and the ant people disappear amid the dust. I panicked: I was here to make sense of myself and my grief, yet with my eyes refusing to work, I couldn't even make sense of my surroundings. My mind was in chaos.

It was evening when I went back to see Mum at the hospital. Frank was already there. Curtains were drawn and the only light in the small room came from a bedside lamp, but I could see that Mum's stare was glazed.

'The doctor injected her with a massive dose of morphine,' Frank said, 'and she's been hallucinating.' The way he spoke made it all sound like some sort of game.

'She didn't want drugs, why did they give her morphine?'

'I don't know, she must have needed it,' Frank replied.

'Are those warts all over your hands?' Mum asked me.

'No!' I replied, initially amused at her deadly serious tone.

'There are bugs on the bed . . . and why is Frank pissing in the corner?' My mum swore! Apart from one time when she'd dropped the vacuum cleaner on her toes she'd never sworn in my presence. 'Look! My skin's turning red!'

'Mum, it's okay, you're not going red. It's just the morphine they've given you that's making you think these things.' But she didn't register what I was saying. I felt horrified, angry and upset, and went to find the doctor.

'Why did you give her morphine? She said she didn't want it and now she's having awful hallucinations.'

'We gave her the drug because she was in great pain,' the doctor replied. I returned to the room feeling very afraid.

'What are you looking at?' I asked, as her gaze followed something.

'Balls dropping from the ceiling,' she answered.

'I'm going home,' Frank said. 'Do you want a lift?'

'No. I'll stay a while longer, but thanks anyway,' I replied. And then it was just us two. Repeatedly raising her arm she grasped at nothing. 'What are you doing?' I asked. I knew I wasn't going to hear anything rational. I just wanted to hear her voice.

'I'm picking loose hairs.' But then, in a moment of lucidity, my mum was back and, looking straight at me, she said, 'I'm scared I'm not going to get out of here.'

I was too. I knew she was going to die. I wondered if she knew it too? Even if she did, I would not confirm both our fears; I revolted against it. My head pounded, my right eye felt like it was going to burst open and tsunami-sized waves of sick dread churned in my guts.

Pounding pain in my head and eyes and a heavy fatigue induced sickness in my guts as I progressed towards the summit of Kilimanjaro. Pushing on and emerging from behind the last of the rocky stacks, I saw a glacier close up for the first time – a sight so remarkable and unexpected that it served as a total distraction from my aching body: stepped blocks of ice whose cliffs, with dirty, geometric upward streaks, creaked and groaned as if in conversation; beyond its icy reaches was the dark silhouette of Mawenzi, a cone of castellated spires. And further away still, where the sky met the horizon, the curvature of the earth was plain to see. Those spellbinding views stopped me in my tracks. When I got going again it hurt to push on to the elusive top, but eventually the rocky path gave way to a trail of footprints over ice-encrusted snow and I knew that I must surely be nearing Uhuru Peak.

Men and women I didn't recognise passed me by, and confusion returned once again to replace the sense of wonderment and peace I'd felt moments before. *They aren't in our group.* 'You're nearly there!' and 'Congratulations!' The American accents twanged, accompanied by a pat on my shoulder.

Who are these people and where have they come from? I asked myself, as I reciprocated their words of encouragement with more a quizzical smile than one of friendly acknowledgement. And as they went on their way I couldn't help but notice they all seemed to have the same sickly yellow complexions. *What's wrong with them?*

We'd walked almost eight hours through the night, but after ten more minutes of determined footsteps, at seven-twenty, I finally made it to the summit. As well as the low hub of noise on approaching Uhuru Peak, the sight of a disorderly queue of human traffic evidenced how busy a mountain Kilimanjaro was. People from a range of nationalities crowded around, waiting for their turn to be photographed next to the sign that proved they'd made it to the roof of Africa. It was surreal. And while strangers hugged and shook hands, all I wanted was for them to disappear. My nerves frayed and finally I lost my temper as Marty started complaining about the water situation again. 'Why don't you take all my food too?' I yelled, and threw a chocolate bar at him before walking away in fury.

The physical effort, the pain, the relief of having made it – everything suddenly threatened to overwhelm me. Desperate to get away from the bizarrely large summit horde, I managed to find a quiet spot where I collapsed to the ground and, with my legs dangling over the rocky shelf, the floodgates opened.

I saw Frank on my way to the hospital that Thursday morning. He stopped his car, rolled down the window and said, 'You know this is it, don't you?'

'No. What do you mean?' I asked.

'The doctor told me your mum is going to slip into a coma.'

Not waiting to hear another word, I raced to the hospital, tears, rage and adrenalin at work. As I reached out to open the door to her room, a warm hand gripped my forearm and I looked up to see who dared stop me. I had been oblivious to the staff in the corridor.

'She won't recognise you,' the doctor warned. 'You must be prepared. She hasn't spoken since last night, and your mum didn't know either me or Frank.' Tears ran down my cold cheeks.

'*Let me go!*' I cried, wrangling free from her grasp and pushing the door open. Mum looked at me with alarm as I almost fell into her room.

'Why are you crying?' she asked, all concerned. Her question caught me off-guard and I experienced a surge of joy amid the agony: I hadn't expected to hear her voice. *They'd said she wouldn't recognise me!*

'I'm not,' I lied as I walked to the window, my back turned so I could quickly wipe tears away.

Composure regained, I sat next to her, telling myself that everything was really all right. Her lips were open, but she didn't speak. I wiped her mouth and I held her. Her eyes stared vacantly. I told her I loved her so many times that if she had been able to register what I was saying I'd have driven her mad. I was quiet when my grandad arrived, and not much later we left – I left her on her own.

'Hi,' she said quietly, when I came back. And then that really was it. She never spoke again.

Grandad brought Gran to the hospital. When he pushed her into Mum's room in a wheelchair the nurse had a hold of Mum under the armpits and was lifting her onto a potty. Mum's nightdress rose, revealing her dark pubis, and though I felt embarrassed at the invasion of her privacy she did not react. I looked at her dumbly. As a child I had sought comfort from that body, whose arms had folded around me and whose hands had clasped mine. As a teenager I'd been grossed out when I'd seen it nude as I'd caught her dressing for work. Her nakedness did not worry me now; it consumed me with sorrow. Hers was a cancer-ravaged frame under a suspended sentence. When Gran saw her daughter, she was overcome; her chest heaved up and down uncontrollably as a tide of emotion burst forth. Rushing from the room to the nearest toilet cubicle, I collapsed onto the floor in my own tearful outpouring. Gran's pain was more than I could bear. I could only imagine how she must have felt to see her child dying. It wasn't right; it wasn't the natural order of things.

Later that evening my grandad returned, red-faced, with several beers inside him. Mum lay catatonic in the hospital bed, and as he gazed at her face and held her hand he softly said, 'My Jeffa', calling her by her pet name. Tears filled my eyes and a lump rose in my throat. And I wondered how many times, and in how many ways, a person's heart could break.

At six o'clock, back at the flat, ringing shredded the dark silence of morning. Its shrill alarm set my heart pounding. I hadn't needed to answer the phone or hear the words: I knew exactly who was calling and why. I went to Frank's room. 'Hurry! We've got to get to the hospital before it's too late.'

I threw on clothes I'd worn the day before and was ready to go, but Frank seemed to take for ever to get ready, and then an infuriating length of time to drive to the hospital. '*Fuck* the speed limit. My mum is dying!' I wailed as the car trundled along at 30mph.

127

It was tempting to open the door, bail out and run as fast as my legs could go: I was desperate to be with her. Frank said nothing.

The overhead lamp was on, its light shone through the tiny frame of glass in the door, and as we entered the room a sweet, sickly scent filled my nostrils. She was lying on her side and her breathing rattled and bubbled, laboured and slowed. I touched her shoulder; her nightshirt was sweat-soaked. I put a disc of classical music that she liked into the CD player, and its vibrations joined the room.

'I wonder where Grandad is?' I said to Frank.

'I told the nurse not to phone him,' he answered.

I felt that my grandfather should have the choice to be there or not, so, going against Frank's decision, I left the room, found a nurse and asked her to make the call. My motives weren't entirely altruistic – *I* needed him there.

Another seeming eternity lapsed before my grandfather arrived. Like Frank he had made himself presentable: my beloved old soldier had washed, shaved, suited up and polished his shoes, and suddenly I felt ashamed to be there in my scabby green mod jacket, jeans and top. Now I detected the faint odour of cigarette smoke from my clothes and hair; my mouth tasted of stale alcohol and I cursed myself for having gone to the pub when I'd left the hospital the night before.

Grandad and Frank each took a chair on either side of my mum's bed while I sat on it and held her hand. We were all quiet, watching, waiting. Barber's *Adagio for Strings* intensified as it crescendoed, and the violins shrieked and screamed as if they knew that the moment had come. Drowning in a cacophony of noise that echoed and thumped in my ears, I wanted it all to be over. I looked at my mum. Weakly, she squeezed my hand.

'It'll be okay. Don't worry. Everything will be all right,' I whispered. *Liar, liar, you big fat fucking liar.* Her eyes stared into the corner of the ceiling, then slowly her head turned. Her gaze shifted to the opposite corner of the room, where it remained fixed. *What's happening? What's she doing? What can she see?* My thumb brushed the bangle on her wrist. *Is it Gerry? Has he come for her?* Her breathing slowed. In ... out ... in ... and that was it. *She isn't taking another breath; where did it go? How can she have just gone?* I could not understand. I searched my grandad's face looking for an answer, but all I saw was sorrow.

Grandad went to find the doctor. 'I've never watched anyone die before,' Frank said flatly as I pressed my cheek against hers: she felt warm. I stroked my hand through the damp curls of her grey hair.

The doctor came in and I had to leave.

I sat on the summit of Kilimanjaro, feeling calmer for a moment. I took out the photograph of me and Mum, and the small pot of her ashes I'd brought. On an impulse, I released them here, so close to her childhood home. Watching her ashes disperse into the crisp mountain air, my memories of her roared with a burning intensity and I felt overcome once more, crying as though she had left me right then.

'I'm sorry,' Marty said, as he came up behind me and put his arms around my shoulders. 'We've been here half an hour. Come on, we need to get down.'

'Okay.' I smiled back. I didn't want to leave, but he was right, our job was only half done. I found a nook in some stones and buried the picture of Mum and me, which I'd popped inside the pot, then stumbled away from Uhuru Peak.

Descent was torturous. And, like the Americans had been, now we were yellow-faced. My mind felt wrecked and all concept of time was lost on me, but I guessed it had to be about ten o'clock when we found ourselves back at Gilman's Point. Kibo's hut and the collection of tents looked tantalisingly close yet were so far away, and now, in the broad light of day, it was startling to see the steepness and distance we had covered during the night. In agonising and fitful bursts of movement I only managed to progress several metres at a time, down loose scree slopes, before having to crouch against or on rocks to catch my breath and let the pain ease.

In the hospital my mother's body lay inert and lifeless, but as I made my way out on the long road towards my grandparents' house it felt as though her spirit had wrapped me up from the inside out like a protective cloak – as though her soul had jumped into my body – and at that moment, in the strangest of ways, I felt comforted. Instead of walking along the pavement I crossed the road, gravitating towards the tall stone boundary wall of the Farmer's Showfield; in my mind I saw it helping to prop me up, preventing me from falling helplessly to my knees. The October wind sent a few rusty-coloured leaves scuttling across my path. The sun pursued its course behind the clouds and the cold, steely grey of day pressed down from all sides, swallowing me whole. Suddenly I understood the meaning of being carefree because I was not, and in crushing defeat I felt as though I never would be again. Each of my footsteps fell automatically, moving my body forward. My body existed but it was as though my spirit, the I that makes me *me*, had transferred to another world where it fluttered unresting and lost. Only my feet progressed towards their destination. At the house I went straight to Gran's room. She was in bed lying up against her pillows. 'Is that it then?' she asked, and Uncle David, seated in the chair next to her, searched my face. Unable to say the words, I walked over, sat across my uncle's knees, put my arms around his neck and cried. I did not see my mother again.

Kibo was a place of safety, and when I finally crashed back into camp I promptly burst into floods of tears again, but this time they were sobs of relief. It didn't matter if I got sick now; I'd achieved the summit. As I pulled myself together, conversation with a tone of concern alerted me to the arrival of a member of our trekking group. His face looked like he lived on a planet with a gravitational pull six times stronger than Earth's; his eyes, and the skin underneath, drooped and sagged, as did his cheeks and the flesh of his jowls. Though supported by a porter, he walked without co-ordination, and his speech was slurred. He'd collapsed on his way back to Gilman's Point and had been out cold. He was an intelligent man (and someone who had taken Diamox from the start) but, driven by summit fever, he had lost all faculty for reason – so much so that he'd put his very life on the line – and it was only my shock at seeing him in that condition that made me appreciate the real danger of climbing at altitude. My thoughts turned to my children. I wanted so much to be with them.

CHAPTER ELEVEN

Dead Loss

Horombo Huts, 3,720 metres, June 2010

I returned to my tent, where I was looking forward to collapsing in a heap, but as I grabbed at the flap to scramble in I came face to face with Marty, who was clearly unwell. He was coughing harshly and his eyes were bloodshot and bulging like a bullfrog's, and with the next bout of coughing he spat blood.

'How long have you been like this?' I asked.

'I was feeling really shit when we were at the summit, but after I left you at Gilman's, that's when the coughing got worse.'

Without hesitation I went to find Emma, who accompanied me back to the tent where she examined my friend. Marty was diagnosed with onset pulmonary oedema, and so while he and the other casualty were raced to lower altitude on one-wheeled contraptions – a metal stretcher, like a mobile see-saw, with handles each end – the rest of us made the four-hour haul on foot.

Trailing down over the vast, dusty expanse, with nothing to see but volcanic boulders and senecio trees, was total and utter hell on earth. I was physically and emotionally spent, had no appetite and was running on empty, but everyone was suffering. All any of us wanted was to reach Horombo camp, and it was a case of every man for himself as people desperately fought to get there. Unsteady on their feet, people fell about; far-spread individuals and pairs staggered along, suddenly dropping to the ground to rest. It was like watching an apocalyptic scene of a film with a cast of zombies, and I was one of them.

Horombo huts eventually came into sight and so did a very chipper Marty; seeing his happy face cheered me up.

'What a speedy recovery! You don't look like Gollum from *Lord of the Rings* any more,' I said.

'Cheeky bitch!' he laughed. 'It's good to see you!'

We chatted for a bit and unpacked the stuff we needed for a last night of camping. Then, after a meagre meal of rice accompanied by carrots and peas (the last of the food supplies), nobody needed persuasion to have an early night – we'd not slept in over thirty-six hours, and any shut-eye prior to that had been in short supply. Bodily weary, I managed only one solitary thought before my eyes closed. *What an epic and twisted forty-eight hours.*

On the first night of life without Mum I barely slept at all. And as I lay in my bed I thought about how I hadn't wanted either the day to finish or time to move forward; and how I hadn't wanted to return to the flat – where she wouldn't be.

I recalled leaving my grandparents' house late and going to visit Mum's friend and teaching colleague, staying with her till midnight – till going home could no longer be avoided. A snippet of Mum's friend's conversation turned over in my mind. 'I remember when she first got breast cancer and your mum said to me, "They found it in my lymph nodes, so that's it, I'm a goner."'

Mum hadn't told me or my grandparents; she had known all along that the cancer would return and that death would come to her sooner rather than later, but she had protected me and all of her family from the truth. A stream of tears trickled from my eyes. I could see my whole life stretching endlessly ahead of me: time was too large and I was swallowed up in it, I didn't want it to go on without her.

It must have been throwing-out time from the pubs because there was sudden noise out in the street. People passing on the pavements below sang, shouted and laughed. I felt resentful and totally disconnected to that world that carried gaily on outside my window. Nobody out there knew how I felt. Nobody out there cared. Why would they? This was my life, my sorrow, and it seemed that nothing would make me feel better ever again.

In the end I gave up on sleep. I reached out for a pile of papers by my bedside on which my mother had handwritten several verses from the *Rubaiyat*. Grandad had given her this book of poetry many years before, and a few weeks earlier she had selected her favourite philosophical quatrains to copy out. She had wanted Grandad and me to find comfort in their words after she was gone. I had coloured Celtic patterns around them, so they had become something we had created together. I lay there looking at them by torchlight, reading those lines over and over again.

Heat from the sun beating through the thin fabric of the tent woke me. My whole head throbbed, my face was puffy, and yesterday's tingling lips had erupted into the mother of all cold sores overnight. But, ropey as I felt, I was determined to make the most of every last minute on Kilimanjaro, a final day of mourning on the mountain, if you like.

Once the breakfast things had been cleared away and before we made tracks down the mountain, the porters and guides put on a final performance for us; they danced and sang their hearts out, cranking up the volume as they belted out the medley of songs that had welcomed us into camp every night. It was a fitting farewell. And afterwards, as we trekked back down beneath the cloud line, I remembered what I could of my mother's last goodbye.

It was hard to recall much about the funeral; the day passed in sketchy scenes. When the hearse drew up outside my grandparents' home my legs virtually gave way beneath me and the world blurred. I don't remember the drive to Inverness, but when we got there I was aware that the crematorium was full to capacity of people who had come to pay their respects, and that was 'nice'. And I vaguely remembered some former pupils of my mother who came to offer up those ritual expressions of consolation. My grandparents, uncles, aunt and Frank maintained composure throughout the service – I don't know how they did it. I wanted to throw myself on top of the box that was taking my mother away. I don't remember the hymns. But I remember the curtains being drawn, then the coffin – with my mum – was gone.

At the wake I drank brandy, because it was what she would have had. I walked – actually, it felt more like I floated – around the tables and in between people. I thought I'd spend the rest of my life feeling permanently numb, so I was pleased to feel a fleeting surge of irritation towards a friend of my grandad's who was filling his face with the sandwiches like he'd come along for the free feed. I wanted to grab his fork and stab his eyeballs, but instead I smiled. I sought out my grandad. Although I felt stone-cold sober, it seemed the alcohol had rubbed out enough brain cells for me to fuck up my attempt at quoting a verse from the *Rubaiyat*, but my grandfather raised his glass with me all the same.

When we arrived back at Nakara Hotel I headed straight for the bar and ordered a brandy, making a toast to my mother and the mountain. As I sipped my drink, though, I felt strangely numb, not at all as I'd expected to feel having conquered the mountain. I had come to Kilimanjaro in hope that the journey to and from its summit would provide the time I needed to make sense of my grief – that by performing my own private memorial, sorrow would vanish as with the wave of a wand, and that by reliving painful memories my inner demons would be cast out. The boundaries of my own endurance had been pushed almost to the limit, so why did I now feel so underwhelmed?

Like everyone else, I continued drinking after dinner, but unlike the others I drank not in celebration of summiting, but to blot out the unbearable fact that my anguish remained. Marty and I got blitzed – I even shared some of his 'bad-boy' grass, giggling uncontrollably for an hour before passing out on my bed.

The undercurrent of disappointment remained as I left Africa behind. As our flight took us further away from Kilimanjaro I tried to work out why the challenge hadn't provided the closure I was after. I'd certainly revelled in the physical and mental punishment the mountain had thrown at me, but once that euphoria had worn off I'd found no lasting change. What now? I remembered my mother's words: *Just keep busy*.

I needed a new focus, a new challenge.

I decided right then that I'd climb all of Scotland's highest mountains, the Munros. I started to feel excited as soon as I'd hit upon this resolve and a sense of renewed hope rose within me.

CHAPTER TWELVE

Peaks and Troughs

The North Glen Shiel Ridge, June 2011

True to my obsessive nature, on my return from Africa I was keen to start ticking off the list of Munros, fixating on reaching the summits of all 284 mountains as quickly as possible. Having taken up a teaching post at a small school near Inverness, I went hillwalking whenever I could find the time.

But despite my frequent excursions, by summer term the following year I felt the familiar tug of anxiety dragging me down again. Though my job was part-time, my evenings were taken up with marking or preparing activities. It seemed I was always rushing to get dinner and bedtimes over with so that I could get on with school stuff. I realised I'd fallen into the very same routine Mum had, and I resented being trapped in a cycle I'd sworn to avoid. Pressures increased when the roof started to leak again, and the uncooperative neighbours at our flat in Nairn continued to cause problems.

In the last months of Mum's life, while she'd still had the energy, she had done up the flat with a view to putting it on the market. We had lived in two homes since moving to the town, the first a tiny one-bedroomed property in the Fishertown area and then a larger flat above the busy High Street. It had more rooms than we really needed, all bright and spacious, but very cold in winter. And because it was an old building it had many problems other than just the freezer-like temperatures.

'I think we should get rid of this place,' she'd said. 'It would be better for you not to have the worry of the leaking roof.'

'No! I don't want you to do that! This is home! It's where we have lived together!' I'd cried.

At that time the idea of selling was inconceivable: my mum was going to die and I didn't want the flat, with our shared memories, taken away from me too. We'd whiled away hours there playing Scrabble or cards. Sitting by the fire reading, or watching TV. Drinking brandy and playing the guitar. We'd fought and made up. She'd helped me with homework to get me through exams, and typed up the dissertation I'd written in my final year at art school. She'd given disastrous cooking lessons in the kitchen: I'd let pans of water burn dry, been heavy-handed with chillies in a curry that blew everyone's heads off, and misunderstanding her instructions I'd drained all the juicy stock from a pan of mince down the plughole.

Mum had been patient and forgiving of me as I struggled to grow up, even when I'd accidentally spilt the bright-red contents of my Indian takeaway all over her new living-room carpet (well, okay, that incurred a three-month silence – but I was easy to ignore since had I scurried off back to art school in Aberdeen feeling very bad and very guilty). I had rarely listened, but Mum had only ever done her best to guide and advise me, and help me become independent. We had been through a lot together in those four walls.

But the flat had been a problem ever since. Recently a large family of Mancunians, minus a wife but plus one dog, had been installed. They were an odd lot and all heavy smokers. Fumes from their cigarettes migrated through the walls, permeating the air, making bedding and clothing in my sons' room smell bad.

Hearing the man's dry cough as he laboured up the communal stairwell one day, I opened my door. He was tall and broad, dressed in baggy jeans and an oversized woolly jumper. I said a breezy, 'Hello.' His unshaven face smiled back and he politely returned the greeting. Maybe I'd stared a little too long, because he then put down his bags and went into a long explanation of why his teeth resembled a broken and rickety picket fence.

'Me teef are needin' fixed. Me wife an' I were rowin' an' she pushed me – I fell into the side of the baffroom door an' all me teef got smashed up,' he said. I lamented their loss and asked what happened with his wife.

'Did you divorce?' I asked.

'No. She's dead. I killed her, but it were an accident. She fell down the stairs.'

'Ooooh!' I said. He began to tell me all the problems he was having with his twenty-year-old daughter and asked if I'd like to come in for a cup of tea sometime. 'Sure,' I answered, then made my excuses and retreated to the flat, deciding I'd complain about his smoke fumes another day.

A few weeks later that strange family did a moonlight flit. Their replacements were just as unpleasant. The regular screaming matches, accompanied by objects being hurled against walls and smashed off floors, were frightening for my younger son to hear, while my older boy was receiving a different kind of education.

'Mum! I can hear them having sex!' Marcus exclaimed as he burst, wide-eyed, through our living-room door.

'Are you sure?'

'Yes, because the lady's saying "Eff me harder!"'

The police were becoming frequent visitors to the residents: they came when there was a fight between the father and son, they came when the man beat his woman and they came to arrest the son, a thief and drug dealer.

Now, despairing of our situation and racked with anxiety, I sat at the kitchen window crying. All my problems were beginning to overwhelm me: the continuous stream of awful neighbours; a personality clash at work; readjusting to life as a single parent. I missed my family and the support they had provided. I felt like such a failure at everything as I sat there punishing myself. I was a shitty, introspective, self-absorbed fuck-up. I hated myself and wanted out of my own skin. I growled with self-loathing till my throat burned. Consumed by loneliness and the burden of my responsibilities, I moved closer to the window and opened it. Leaning forward, I peered down into the darkness, gripped suddenly by a terrible urge to leap. *Be spontaneous! Don't think about it, just do it. It'll all be over quickly!* It was a fleeting thought. I knew I could never do it, never deliberately choose to leave my little boys. I would put on a brave face for them and carry on going.

I needed the breathing space that I only found on the hills to help me cope, but in my agitated state I began to hit them harder, becoming increasingly careless.

At seven-thirty in the morning the alarm on my mobile went off. I'd arranged to meet Ollie in Inverness; we were heading north-west to do four Munros on the north Glen Shiel Ridge. After our first meeting on Meall a' Bhuachaille in 2008, Ollie and I had been out walking together a number of times and were now pretty comfortable in each other's company. Our association was uncomplicated; we met for hillwalks and kept conversation light-hearted. Ollie saw me as a joker, but humour, for a long time, had been a front. Underneath it, a sense of angry frustration had taken over. Like a midnight tide that washes in, depression seeped its inky darkness through me as I struggled on.

Now, as Ollie drove us to our next challenge, I lowered my seat and closed my eyes, listening to the rain as it pattered off the windows.

It had been a rainy day, four weeks after Mum's funeral, when I was manhandled back into Woolworths by security. I was led up some stairs, their tan colouring worn down to a smooth grey in the centre of each step. What a truly unimportant thing for my stumbling mind to have focused on. A grubby white door was pushed open and I was taken into a small office. Dressed in a navy-blue pullover and skirt, the manageress, a dumpy woman with a terrible mousey-blonde perm and huge framed glasses, sat behind a desk that was covered in piles of paper in messy stacks. There were files and boxes everywhere, more like how I imagined the office of a journalist or private detective might be – except here there were random toys and Christmas decorations lying about. She'd phoned the police and officers were on their way. My belly churned, my head felt light and my brain raced at a rate of knots as the consequences of my actions finally sunk in. *What in the fuck were you thinking? You have money. You could have paid. You even realised the security guy was watching you. Why didn't you just dump the stuff? You're such an idiot.* I then recoiled as horror filled me. What were my grandparents going to think?

The door opened and in walked a policeman. I looked up at his face, which was partially concealed under the shiny peak of his black cap, and cringed. I couldn't believe it. I knew him. My embarrassment doubled as my mind flickered back to the night I'd shagged him down the putting green, long ago. I kept quiet but I knew he recognised me too. He opened up the large, white-plastic carrier bag that I'd stashed the stolen goods in and pulled the bizarre variety of items out one by one. He looked at me, and then at the manageress.

'I think', he said, 'that in this case it would probably be better if you don't press charges. I know Sarah's circumstances and, if she is agreeable, I would instead refer her to the community psychiatric team for counselling.'

There was a pause before the manageress nodded.

'I don't want to see you in my store again,' she warned sternly.

'Okay,' I answered, and then asked if my name would appear in the paper.

'No. We can keep you out of that,' the policeman answered.

'Thank you,' I said, grateful that my grandparents would be spared the knowledge and shame of what I'd done. And with that I was free to leave.

Yet I was not free.

I hadn't been able talk to my grandparents about how I really felt inside. How could I? I knew that their hearts were as broken as mine. I'd lost my mum, but they'd buried their child. I could only imagine their suffering. And yet they sheltered me from their own pain with a united show of composure. I witnessed only one outpouring of grief, from my grandfather. It was my fault, I'd said something, I can't even remember what, that finally broke through his stoic self-control. He jumped up from his chair in the living room, banged his fists on the wall and cried, 'I can't seem to say anything right!' His outburst was so unexpected, so out of character, I was completely taken aback. Guilt pinned me to my seat on the sofa, hating myself for being the cause of this dreadful moment, for hurting him.

Other than that brief eruption, though, my grandparents 'soldiered on'. Their strength and depth of character was humbling, so I hid my shoplifting shame and pretended that I was strong too – and, besides, it would only have caused them concern and even more upset if they'd known. So we three carried on with our usual routines, each suffering alone in silence. My brush with the law had given me a fright, but it didn't change the blackness inside that I believed was going to drive me insane with grief, turn me into an alcoholic or, more likely, both. It was not a good place to be. And as the rain came down, I thought maybe it wasn't a bad thing that I was going to have to see to a counsellor.

It was a two-hour journey before Ollie and I, having driven through Glen Shiel, arrived at Morvich, a tiny settlement near the southern end of Loch Duich. The rain had stopped, though the sky remained heavy as we turned off the road and parked beyond a large metal gate. Feeling tired and sluggish, I put on my gaiters and waterproof jacket and set out on the six-kilometre route to Glen Licht House. Silver puddles filled the potholes on the stony dirt track that ran alongside the River Croe, its peat-coloured waters cutting a meandering path through the bottom of this wide, treeless valley. The lower slopes of the great mountain ridges that hemmed us in on both sides were cloaked in a deep and luscious green, fresh from the summer rains. Higher up, rocks glistened. Shreds of light found a way through rolling folds of gunmetal cloud and fell like ripples on the mountainside. The atmospheric trickery made it impossible to tell exactly how steep parts of these mountains were, but I had no doubt we were in for quite the slog upwards. It was only when we reached the isolated building at the end of the track that I realised I'd neglected to factor in the distance and time it had taken to walk those extra kilometres – adding another two and a half hours to what was already going to be a lengthy day. I felt cross with myself and worried that it would be near ten o'clock that night before I got home to the kids. Their grandparents hadn't been able to help on this occasion, and so the boys were being looked after by Sam. Although our marriage had long since been over we had remained in touch and he sometimes helped me out with them – the boys were familiar with him, and Sam was still fond of them too.

We followed a good path, in a southerly direction, alongside a tributary stream that we needed to cross. Heavy rains had made the river lively, and a suitable place to cross difficult to find. But it was after I had slipped off some rocks and got my feet wet that my temper escalated beyond the combined heights of the mountains we were scaling. Ollie, for reasons only he knew, decided to do a gigantic zigzag up unforgivingly steep and craggy terrain in the opposite direction to the line I'd mapped out. And I followed him. A southerly wind, now blowing fiercely, brought low cloud and light rain, making it feel all the more like hard work to get anywhere.

It now seemed I couldn't even get to the top of a hill without messing up. Depression was not meant to follow me on the mountains. I yelled my frustration and rage into the wind till my throat hurt and tears burned. Ollie was too far ahead to have heard me wailing like a lunatic, and in any case the strong winds blowing against us carried the din away in the opposite direction.

A day after the incident at Woolworths I took Poppy for a walk. I was desperate to reach the white sands of Nairn's east beach, knowing that at this time of the year it was unlikely there would be anyone about. I'd chosen the place deliberately, so that I could scream out all the anger and misery and pain from the top of my lungs.

A man appeared from between sand dunes, looking distinctly alarmed when he'd heard my cry.

'Are you all right?' the poor unsuspecting soul asked.

No, not really. My mother is dead, I got done for shoplifting the other day and I want to fucking top myself.

'Yes,' I stammered, 'I'm fine.'

The man walked on uncertainly, and I felt idiotic. Nevertheless, as soon as I was alone on the wide, open space of the beach I started talking to myself again, pretending Mum was walking with me. *'I dreamt about you last night. You told me that there is a heaven and everyone gets to go there. You said you'd done more there in two days than you could do in a lifetime on Earth . . . I wish I always got to see you in my dreams . . . I miss you so badly Mum.'*

I walked for empty miles along the sand till the chill December wind made my fingers, toes and lips as numb as I felt on the inside. And I remembered the promise I'd made not to give up. Sea air blustered across cold, grey waters carrying a gull's cry. Looking to the sky, I said to Mum, *'I'll speak to the counsellor. I'll do teacher training. I'll go see your friend and ask if she'll let me have work experience in her class. I won't steal, I won't drink and I won't let you down again, Mum. I'll be better.'*

After the shoplifting incident I hadn't said anything to my grandparents about having to see a counsellor, but there were some things that could not be left unsaid. I hadn't been feeling right since my walk on the beach. There was something more than grief going on inside me. With all the upset I hadn't even noticed I'd missed a period, but at a doctor's appointment it was confirmed I was pregnant. Dr Collier had been our family's doctor for years. It was she who had been on duty at the hospital when Mum was dying; her warm hand that had held me back, and her voice that warned me that Mum might not recognise me. She had always been so kind, I trusted her and could tell her things I couldn't speak to my grandparents about. When, years later, she told me she was retiring, I was devastated. 'Who am I going to talk to now?' was all I managed to say.

Now, as she delivered the news of my impending motherhood, a range of emotions pulled me in every direction. What was I going to do? After losing my mum there was no way I wasn't keeping my baby. But I was scared to tell my grandparents. Of the two it was Gran I chose to tell first. My boyfriend and I had already parted company with no chance of reconciliation, so I knew my grandfather was going to be even more disapproving, but to have Gran onside would cushion the anticipated blow of his reaction. Behind Grandad's slim facade was a man to be reckoned with. Not that he ever ranted or raved – it was the disappointment visibly etched on his face combined with a quiet but disparaging remark, and an exit from your presence, that left you wanting to crawl away, tail between legs, feeling abysmal for having let him down. I was dreading it. 'So . . . will you tell Grandad for me?' I'd asked.

'She's pregnant,' Gran said when Grandad entered the bedroom with her dinner; subtlety had never been her strong point. He thrust the tray of food onto her lap and left without casting so much as a glance in my direction. It had been expected, but it still hurt. Sitting on the dusky-pink tweed-covered armchair next to her bed, I looked at Gran.

'I suppose he thinks like mother like daughter,' I said, my voice cracking.

'Don't worry. He'll come round. He did with your mum and he will with you.' Gran's friendship was invaluable to me. She talked about my grandad and the fun they used to have. A flicker of youth shone in her old eyes as she'd told me about an officers' party, and how the men had to put their wives over their shoulders and race to the end of the hall. 'But your grandad was so skinny that I picked him up and carried him instead,' she said with a little chuckle. 'I think that was the night he pushed me home in a shopping trolley.' Gran was a marvel. She must still have been feeling grief-stricken too, but told me her stories – her way of letting me know I was loved by them both. That night I prayed to the God that my grandad had faith in, the God I wanted to believe in.

'Help us through these times. Look after my gran and my grandad. Thank you for giving me my baby.' As I lay in bed, in the darkness of my room, I knew that the new life growing inside would save me from myself.

It took Ollie and me a further three hours to reach the first summit. With every step, I'd finally felt my black mood slowly slipping away, the soothing familiarity of the mountain scenery and the effort of the physical exertion gradually softening the turmoil of my raw emotions until all traces of my usual pain and anguish had been erased altogether.

'You know why I love mountains, Ollie? 'Cause they make me feel great!' I announced cheerfully when I caught up with him.

The wind continued to blow hard, but we snatched glimpses of our surroundings from clearing views. It was a magnificent, time- and weather-worn landscape I saw as I looked south-west across to the unmistakable long, straight ridge of Sgurr na Sgine, presenting visibly beneath the cloud line. In thick clag we made our way along the ridge and congratulated each other when we arrived at the top of the second Munro. I shrieked our silly summit catchphrase, 'Nippy tunnel!', as we balled our fists, bumped knuckles with each other, beat our chests and punched the sky. It was only after performing another nippy tunnel, and when we came upon an impressively stacked third cairn, that we realised we were at the actual, genuine, bona-fide second summit. We laughed and blamed our mistakes on the weather.

Thick, white mists enfolded us as we wandered away from the peak on a path that led out along an ever-narrowing rocky spine. It was a good forty minutes later and after losing some height that I began to notice the landscape did not look as it should. I showed Ollie the map and he agreed, 'We're on the wrong bloody ridge!' Even though I knew what to do with a map and compass, in poor conditions I realised how easy it was to go wrong. Small mistakes could end in big disaster; the mountains were no place for complacency.

'I'm really sorry,' I said, feeling bad again, but by half past five I was dancing on the third summit, overcome with happiness once more. The cloud had lifted and I was confident there would be no more mistakes. And even another sweat-inducing, calf-killing haul up over a couple of false tops to reach the day's fourth and final Munro only served to enliven my spirit. Ollie was lagging behind, but with the incredible views of the ridge we'd just walked and the spectacular peaks of the Glen Affric mountains to the north, I was in my element.

'I won't lie, Sarah,' Ollie said as he made it to the top, 'I'm knackered!'

'At least it's all downhill from here,' I grinned.

A path from the summit petered out to give way to nature's own carpet of grasses, moss and flowering mountain plants, butterwort and tiny purple orchids. In the distance, the bright-red roof of a small building down in the valley was where we set our sights; it didn't seem that far. Well, we walked and we walked, but we didn't seem to be drawing any nearer to it. The ground was becoming soggier. Shooting pain surging through my right knee made the descent feel unending, and it was always a downer to know that I was returning home to the same old worries.

L ife had been a journey of peaks and troughs, but that first year without Mum was hard. Frank and I wanted to keep her close so the urn containing her ashes remained in the flat. Two months after Mum died, on Christmas Eve, I'd spent the day with my grandparents and it was teatime before I went home. I wanted to talk to my mum but her ashes, which we'd put on the mantelpiece in the living room, weren't there. Without having said a word or left a note, Frank had taken her away. My heart raced as I assumed the worst. We hadn't been getting along and I thought that he had gone to scatter her ashes without me. Through choked tears I repeatedly tried to get hold of him by phone, but got no answer. I called Uncle David.

'Have you seen Frank?'

'No,' he replied.

I called Frank's number again, and this time he picked up.

'Where have you taken my mum?' I asked, trying to suppress the anger and grief that raged inside.

'I just took her for a walk. That's all,' he answered.

It was years later when he finally told me that he'd taken the urn with her ashes to Beinn Eighe, that beautiful high loch in Wester Ross. He had meant no harm, but that Christmas Eve I hated him for making me panic like that. Too wrapped up in my own grief, I didn't stop to consider his.

After that, I saw the counsellor twice a month for six months and at first I tried to articulate my feelings, but it didn't seem to be helping – I never really felt I could connect with the woman. So I told her the things she wanted to hear and took my own measures in the battle against the blackness. I made endless lists and set goals. But all the while I swung like a pendulum: from aching heights of gratitude and hope when I heard my unborn child's heartbeat or felt his kick, to the miserable depths of tears and headaches; of brushing my face with a lock of Mum's hair; or holding her nightshirt, the one she had worn during those last hours in hospital, to breathe in the faint smell of her life. All her other clothes had been boxed up and given to charity; I had never before been a worshipper of things, but the presence of her life was solidified in those strands of her hair and in her nightshirt.

Cries for my mum during labour pains in the hospital were heard only by the four walls, but when my son was born and I cradled him for the first time, I was possessed by overwhelming love.

The immediate responsibility I felt for my son helped me understand better how my grandparents had managed their grief when they'd lost their daughter. They weren't superhuman: they'd put on a brave face and were strong because they'd had to be for the rest of their family, for me. Through my tears I whispered into my baby's ear, 'Your grandma would love you!'

CHAPTER THIRTEEN

A Hatch and Despatch

Bidein a' Choire Sheasgaich
and Lurg Mhor, October 2011

I'd had a bad bout of flu, but despite my illness, and the constant downpours, winds and the cold, nothing had stopped me from knocking out twelve Munros over the course of an extended weekend. Incapable of slowing down and indifferent to the weather, I kept heading out on long mountain days, even though hours of daylight were shortening. And after another big outing, on the Mamores, I made plans for the following day to tackle two of the most isolated Munros in the country.

After catching five hours' sleep I was up and getting organised when there was a soft rap on the door. It was Marty. We had kept in contact after Kilimanjaro and he had offered to join me on my walk today.

'Morning! Your bike's in the jeep. I even pumped your tyres up; how were you gonna ride it wi' flats, ya tube? You ready?' He said.

'Yup,' I grinned.

'How far is the walk anyway?' he asked as we drove north.

'Twenty-nine kilometres. I reckon it'll take us ten hours tops,' I answered confidently. 'If we can set off at half-eight we should be down before it's too dark.'

'Well, sunset's at quarter to six. You got your headtorch?' he asked.

'Yeah, course I do,' I replied.

'Good. 'Cause I forgot mine,' he said. I shook my head and laughed.

At quarter past eight we arrived at Craig, four kilometres east of Achnashellach in the north-west of Scotland. Rain fell steadily. Crossing the railway line, we continued by bike on a wide, stony track bordered by trees, but I soon dismounted and pushed while Marty bust his competitive guts, cycling the steep uphill, to the deer fence.

Forty-five minutes later we had dumped our wheels and were following a trail towards a wooden rope bridge that I'd used once before to cross the river. To our dismay we found the rope lying in a curled mass by the piers, but luckily the water wasn't in spate, and protruding boulders provided a way over. Tired from the previous days of walking, my legs were like lead as we hiked up the stalkers' path, but we chattered non-stop, making the time it took to reach the col pass relatively quickly. Marty was being all profound, telling me how he thought he'd finally met the right girl.

'In the past, when I've been in a relationship, I've always been looking for something better. Sometimes you have to stand back and take notice of what's staring you in the face,' he said. 'You not met anyone yet?'

'Na. There's no way I'm getting involved with anyone any-time soon,' I answered cheerfully. But inside I felt rueful. I'd never chosen well, always in a rush to find love and ending up in the wrong relationships, then staying involved for too long out of a misguided determination that I could make it work. After so many failures, I found it hard to believe I could ever really have a successful relationship.

Bells had rung in a new year and a new millennium, and life somehow carried on without Mum. Although the undercur-rent of sadness remained, Marcus, now a toddler, brought me lots of happiness, and a return to bar work also helped me to smile and joke again. And then I met Charlie. I'd gone down to the fruit and veg shop, and, spotting me struggling as carrier bags swung from each handlebar, Charlie offered to hold my bike so that Marcus could stay in the child seat while I got my goods and paid at the counter. I was immediately taken with him as I overheard him chatting away to my son, and I was flattered by the attention he paid me too. From there, things moved quickly and, desperate for love and companionship, I soon fell for him.

One evening, as we were making love in the dark, he let out a yelp and gripped my arms. 'Sarah! Stop moving!' His distress alarmed me, and I wondered what the hell was wrong as I hov-ered above him. 'Your earring! It's caught up my nose!' he cried. The silver hoop had unclasped, catching his nostril like a fish on a hook. Releasing him from its sharp grip, I ruptured into uncon-trollable peals of laughter. It was the first real belly laugh I'd had since my mum died, something I had never thought could happen.

When I finally wore myself out, a wave of disgust washed over me as I registered that my laughter had briefly obliterated my grief.

Charlie and I started to see more of each other, but I kept it quiet from my grandparents at first. He was seven years younger than me, which I knew they wouldn't approve of, and in any case I wasn't sure if the relationship would amount to anything, so there didn't seem any point in upsetting them for no reason. Besides, my grandfather's mood had been low, and a combination of various ailments gave poor old Gran more than a few good reasons for her increasing despondency. I didn't think it would be helpful to add to their stress by introducing a boyfriend I knew they would consider unsuitable.

In the two years since Mum had died I'd seen my grandparents most days. I'd sit with my grandad in the kitchen then pop into Gran's room. We'd chat or just watch one of her programmes on TV, but there had been an evident shift in her mood. She had, completely out of character, stopped eating and would only sip at drinks. She'd gone silent too, and I had the horrible feeling she was dying. Panic set in. Sitting on the chair next to her bed, desperate for any conversation, I showed Gran the funny picture on a birthday card I'd bought. 'That's a very painful operation, I've seen it on the telly,' she said.

'She was meant to have laughed,' I said to my grandfather when I saw him later. He shared my concern.

'She asked me how much the dog cost and when I asked her what she meant she replied, "Well, I thought you were taking the dog to the vets because she smells?"' Then he added, 'I think she's going a bit ga-ga. And the multiplicity of pills pushed into her by the doctors do little to help. I'm afraid there isn't anything much we can do for her, she doesn't want any of her usual goodies, not even a small slice of my lemon cheesecake,' he said.

I grabbed Poppy's lead and took her out. 'If I'm ever on a life-support machine,' Gran had once said, *'don't* switch me off!' Mum, Gran and I had all laughed together at her statement, but we knew she meant it. She was a woman who clung ferociously to life, which made it all the harder to bear witness to her decline. When I returned with the dog I was greeted at the door by the doctor, who was just leaving.

'An ambulance is on its way,' Grandad said. 'Your gran is going to the local hospital.' I knew exactly what that meant. Her body was giving up and she was too.

Later that evening I called in to see her. Two-year-old Marcus and Poppy were with me.

'Can you stay in the corridor please while we clean up your gran and give her an injection? It won't take long,' a nurse requested.

Waiting at the door, I stared at the room opposite. *Last time I was here I was in that room. Mum died in there. Poor Gran, she'll remember that too; why'd they have to put her here?* I thought sombrely. A smiling nurse left the door ajar, indicating that I could go in. And so there I stood at the end of her bed.

'Has your grandad left?' she said.

'Yes,' I answered. *He must have been here earlier.*

Pouring some Coke into a glass, I gave it to her to sip. Her fight was gone. She wasn't interested in the words coming from my mouth. She just stared as though lost in her own deep thought.

'I'll be off now. Grandad will be in later, so I'll see you tomorrow,' I said as cheerfully as possible, but feeling great anguish.

She looked straight at me then, with softness in her eyes as she opened them right up, like she was taking in one last good look at me. A momentary flicker of a smile was directed at Marcus, who sat placidly in his backpack. I wanted to say, 'I love you', but to do that would have felt too much like confirmation that I might never see her again.

At half past ten the next morning the phone rang. It was my aunty. 'Mum died in the early hours.'

'No!' I cried, 'I've got to go to her!'

Leaving Marcus with my grandad, I went to the hospital. I made my way along the corridor to Gran's room, where she lay as though sleeping. *Why didn't anyone tell me? I'd never have let you leave on your own.* My heart shattered again, and my entire being trembled. Sitting in the chair by her bed, I took her hand in mine and stroked it. Her pale, paper-thin skin felt silky, but ice-cold – not warm like my mum's had been. I reached my arm across her body and rested my head on her chest. Unexpectedly, Gran burped. Jumping out of my skin, I withdrew from the embrace. I looked at her . . . *no . . . she is definitely still dead* . . . and then I started laughing through my tears.

For the second time I found myself in a black car being driven to the crematorium, as 'Marble Halls', the only tune I knew Gran liked, played over and over inside my head. In two years I had lost the two most significant women in my life. In a trance-like state I stared from the car's window onto a grey and silent world.

Black-headed gulls with motionless wings were being carried on the wind. I envied those gulls right then.

It was only one month after Gran died when I found out I was expecting my second child.

Concluding that there would never be a 'right time' to tell my grandad, I'd decided to bite the bullet and announce my pregnancy. In light of losing Gran I was sure the news couldn't make him feel too much worse, but all the same I wasn't expecting a pat on the back and a 'Well done, dear.'

Steeling myself, I entered Grandad's kitchen.

'What?' he spat, in disbelief. 'Tell me, are there going to be five different fathers waiting at the park for their children in another five years' time?' His words cut me down, and this time there was no Gran to hide behind. But I refused to skulk off. *He'll come round*.

I visited my grandfather most days, helping out around the house, making dinner and going on the supermarket run. And of an evening I'd return to take the dog out. Often I'd walk into the living room to find him sitting in dim light with a whisky by his side, gazing up at a black and white photograph of his four young children. 'I like to look at my little family, sitting there together on the sofa, all smiles,' he'd say. I sensed his sorrow, and knew he missed both Mum and Gran.

At the end of the millennium year Leon was born by caesarean section. At the same time, the prediction my grandfather had made – that the relationship with the baby's father was destined for failure – was about to come true. On New Year's

Eve, when I should have been celebrating the latest addition to my little family, I discovered that Charlie was seeing someone else.

My grandad, who had come to visit, found me bent double and weeping at the top of the communal stairwell.

'What on earth is the matter, Sarah?' he asked.

'I've hurt myself,' I answered. That was partly true. I'd been outside to fetch some coal, and the exertion of carrying its weight so soon after my operation had been too much. But we both knew that wasn't why I was crying.

'You shouldn't be lifting heavy things. Let me,' he said, taking the buckets of coal, 'and then you can tell me what's really wrong.' In a reversal of roles, my octogenarian grandfather ended up looking after me.

M y grandfather had been my last source of support when I was feeling vulnerable. Now, with all of them gone, I often felt as if I had no one to turn to. At least on the mountains I could count on my walking companions. Out with Marty, I felt much more confident than I would have done on my own in this wilderness. I knew that any problems the mountain threw at us we would solve together.

Taking a bearing at the col, Marty and I tackled the Corbett, which stood between us and the first Munro. At its summit we followed the twisting, bumpy ridge and as we reached its end I spied a massive drop to the next narrow col between the Corbett and Munro, and rising behind that was a forbidding and seemingly sheer wall of rock.

Mists engulfed us and it was difficult to see much other than the immediate vertical crags. We picked up a path, only for it to lose itself in the wall. We wasted a lot of time trying to find a way up the broken cliffs, but contouring the mountain westwards we found a mossy breach in the hill's defences and began to pull ourselves up. Great clumps of loose earth came away in our hands and underneath our feet the terrain slipped away, forcing us to move quickly up crags and gullies. Wind and rain were making the going more challenging, but Marty's banter kept me distracted till we finally topped out. It had taken us five and a half hours – too long. But, after walking around the west side of a high lochan and up a neatly tapering ridge, we were at the summit.

'Man, cheesecake mountain was hard earned,' I panted.

'Cheesecake?' Marty said, his chin retracting into his neck and his nose wrinkling.

'Yeah. Cheesecake. I can never pronounce this mountain's Gaelic name, cheesecake is close enough!'

'Ha, yeah. Cheesecake. It was a beast,' Marty agreed. 'Listen; if we don't hit the second Munro within the next forty-five minutes I think we should turn round. Time's not on our side,' he said. I reluctantly agreed. Keeping on the move, we stepped up the pace.

The route to Lurg Mhor was easier, and, covering ground on a good path, we made its top in the timescale we'd agreed. Marty stuffed his face while I managed only one bite of my roll. My appetite had deserted me, but I didn't think twice about it. It was only as we were retracing our steps and I began to feel sick that I realised I hadn't eaten much all day – Marty had arrived early that morning, and in the sudden rush to get out I had completely forgotten to grab anything for breakfast. I'd already started our day feeling physically drained and by the time we were back at the first summit I was consciously battling against waves of nausea brought on by fatigue. I said nothing. The lochan we'd passed earlier was now sunlit, and to the west were dazzling views over other sparkling high lochs. Down-climbing the rocky wall came easily as we picked up a path east of the lochan, and as Marty whistled I felt a second wind and started to feel brighter.

At quarter past five we were back at the summit of the Corbett. We came down at first on a path but then over rough ground to what we assumed was the col. Neither of us checked the map. We dropped down some more. Dark cloud thickened overhead. And at half past five we realised something was wrong. We'd come off the Corbett too soon. Checking the map, we agreed to keep contouring around and down, but discovered we were walking towards broken cliffs whose drops were big enough to cause serious injury if we were to go over the edge. Light was disappearing fast and the terrain underfoot was difficult: slippery rocks were separated by squelchy bog and heathery mounds as we detoured to avoid the dangers of the crags. It began to rain steadily again and I knew then that we were in for a long night. We slid and stumbled our way across the rough ground, and Marty took a couple of hard falls onto rock, but we finally made the bealach (the pass between the hills) and in pitch-blackness walked out on the stalkers' path. Small but noisy rivers now gushed across the path everywhere and suddenly I felt the bulk of those surrounding black mountainous bodies closing in, squashing me. My head went light and I fell to the ground.

'Holy shit. You okay?' Marty's voice echoed over me.

'Don't feel so good,' I whispered, sticking my head between my knees.

'Here take this, it'll help,' he said, pulling a bottle from his bag and then me to my feet. There was no choice but to keep walking. 'Back in my navy days,' Marty said, pausing dramatically, 'we danced the sailors' hornpipe.'

He blethered a whole heap of crap to take my mind off what we were doing, and as he talked the rain stopped. The clouds broke up to reveal the Milky Way stretching across the heavens, and more and more points of light appeared above our heads. A beautiful end to our fourteen-hour day.

Shortly before midnight, after an hour's drive to the nearest fast-food stop, Marty quizzed me as he stuffed fries into his mouth.

'How you feeling now?'

'In pain!' I answered truthfully, 'but it's my own fault.' Every bit of my mouth was agony as I mashed a small bite of burger between my molars – the hangover from my illness on the mountain. 'I should have forced some food down earlier, I didn't realise I was running on empty,' I groaned. 'I won't make that mistake again.'

I'd become used to learning from my blunders out on the mountains. There had been an element of uncalculated fright in most of my recent outings. But I'd found overcoming each stressful situation emboldening and addictive. I enjoyed the challenges and being pushed out of my comfort zone. I still hadn't reached the limits and that was exciting, because it meant there was more to come. There was no feeling like it: to experience my own vulnerability and master it. But despite my determination not to make any more mistakes, the mountains were about to teach me the most important lessons of my life, and I was heading for a fall.

CHAPTER FOURTEEN

Slippery Slopes

Near Fersit, January 2012

It was the last day of January 2012 when Ollie and I arrived at Fersit, a remote hamlet between the Cairngorm National Park and Fort William. Clouds were gathering ominously. Bitter cold hit my face as I got out of the car and something nagged inside as I looked in the direction of Stob Coire Sgriodain and Chno Dearg, the mountains we were going to climb.

Ascending a gentle gradient across moorland of heathers and grasses, I stopped momentarily to take a photograph of a small stream whose tiny waterfall was rendered motionless by winter's spell. Continuing for more than an hour over rough ground, we reached the foot of a steep, craggy nose. We decided to climb up one of its snow-filled gullies. Off I went up the glistening-white chute, my crampons biting into the icy terrain with a reassuring crunch. Twenty feet ahead I was feeling smug as I stopped and looked back at my flailing companion.

'You really ought to invest in crampons, Ollie,' I shouted as I took his photograph, while thinking up some smart-ass comments to tag onto the pictures.

'I'm going to aim for the rockier bit; I'll see you up there,' he called.

Traversing across the steep slope, I realised not all points on my crampons were making contact with the snow; I was like a car taking a corner on two wheels and my weight wasn't being distributed effectively. The nagging feeling returned. With my next step the crampon on my left foot bit in, but without enough purchase, and as I raised my right foot, *whoosh!* I was on my backside and sliding fast. I couldn't self-arrest because my ice axe was lying in the boot of the car.

'*OLLIE, OLLIE!*' I yelled.

And then I did what I knew I shouldn't do. I used my foot as a brake. The metal spikes bit in and stuck fast, but momentum and gravity continued to propel my body forwards. My body flipped over and, with a mouthful of freezing snow, I eventually came to a grinding halt. My ankle felt useless, hot and traumatised.

'Have you got your mobile? You need to call for help,' I said as Ollie approached.

'Do you want to see if we can get you to flatter ground?'

'There's no way I can move. I think it's broken . . . I'll try.' But the foot did nothing at my command. 'You definitely need to make the call,' I groaned.

Putting on my down jacket, I also wrapped myself as best I could in my orange bothy bag and lay on my tilted frozen bed, propped up by my elbows for support. Scared I would start sliding again, I concentrated my efforts on not losing grip.

'If I'd kept going and hit my head I could be dead,' I said, as I looked at the rocks below.

'Aye, how many lives is that you've got left now?'

'Do you know what I'm most mad about . . . no more hillwalking for me for at least six months. I'm such an idiot.'

There was nothing I could do but wait for the helicopter and try to find strength in the face of a difficult situation – as I had done before.

G ran was gone. With his old routine abandoned, time was my grandad's own. He'd spent his entire life looking after his family, so I said nothing when I saw that he had started on the whisky a little earlier in the day. If anything was giving me cause for concern it was his frailty.

He had always had a slight frame. Poking fun, we'd call him a skinny freak. But during the course of his life my grandfather had suffered a great deal of physical hardship. I remember sitting at the dinner table as a kid when he announced, and not without surprise himself, that the ulcers he had been going back and forth to hospital about for the past ten years had actually been stomach cancer. He said that when the doctors gave him the all-clear that day they told him they hadn't expected him to survive six months and called him a miracle.

After my mother died Grandad told me a story that gave me a rare glimpse into his past. 'I was on campaign in Tobruk, in North Africa, during the Second World War when we were captured and transported on an awful ship from Egypt to Italy. On the first day we were given one square biscuit each and a little water, the second day half a biscuit and the third day even less. All of us were cramped in the bottom of the ship. And when we arrived at the prisoner-of-war camp in Italy we were starved for months on end,' he said. 'That's why it annoys me when people say they are starving. Most of them don't have a clue what that is.' He referred to those times as 'the sad days'.

Skin and bone he was, but mentally my grandfather had always been strong and sharp as a tack – I reckoned it was all down to his army training and the daily ritual of his crossword. Friends referred to him as 'Gentleman Jim', and those who had received his epistles often said his command of the English language was almost Churchillian. He was a man who chose his words wisely. And in times of crisis those words were heartfelt and always in the right tone. But now, with each passing week and month he was losing a bit more of his mental faculty. He didn't fuss, and candidly blamed old age for absent-mindedness. But it was the transition from small, innocuous things, like not being able to finish the crossword to being found wandering around near the river when he had forgotten his way home that raised serious misgivings. The doctor diagnosed dementia.

Between us, my aunt and I did our best to care for my grandad, and I continued to walk the dog. An increasingly unenthusiastic Poppy would greet me with a half-hearted wag of her tail when I called to take her out, preferring, more often than not, to lie prostrate at the threshold of Grandad's room, her large, sandy bulk impossible to budge. Like Gran, she too went off her food and, an old girl herself, it wasn't long before she had to be put to sleep.

Seasons changed. Winter approached. A few nasty slips on frosty pavements resulted in my grandad being carted off to hospital in an ambulance, blood gushing from his head or his hands. But the colder weather brought other health troubles. One afternoon when I called to the house, Grandad was asleep in bed. Wine gums he'd been sucking had dribbled from his mouth and now stuck like medals to the sleeve and shoulder of his shirt. His lungs were rattling and he sounded in a bad way, so I called the doctor out; he suspected pneumonia. An ambulance came once again. At hospital Grandad hallucinated a lot; he thought he could see soldiers marching over a hill and a little boy crying, but when he tried to comfort the child the boy slipped further away. I wondered if he was the little boy. Pulling through the worst of the illness, he looked at me as he lay half propped up in the hospital bed.

'Why didn't you just let me go?' he said. Tears pricked my eyes.

'Because I love you so much,' my voice cracked. I felt guilty and selfish, and I hurt enormously.

My grandad now needed round-the-clock care and so arrangements were made for him to move into a nearby nursing home – the last place he'd wanted to end up. I felt I'd let him down: by making him live, and then because of his incarceration. I went to see him almost every day and would read to him from the *Rubaiyat*. Even if he didn't take it in, I found solace in its verses – just as my mother had intended.

Another cold January passed and Aunty Penny and I continued to pay regular visits to the nursing home, but Grandad hadn't been doing so well. One day a member of staff called to ask me to come over. 'I'm sorry, but he won't pull through this time,' the doctor said.

His words had the same effect as if he'd taken his fist and punched it straight through my guts. I arranged for the boys to stay with their paternal grandparents, packed a toothbrush and some clothes, and later that evening I returned to the nursing home. The boys and I had the rest of our lives together. Right now my place was with my grandad. He was my last connection to my past, to my mother. I loved him so much I couldn't bear to leave his side, and so I slept on the floor by his bed for four nights – and I slept better in the home than I had at the flat. I didn't need to worry about the phone ringing with bad news; and I was protected from the wild running of my imagination, because I was there. During the day, carers popped in to change Grandad's clothes and he would silently and obediently comply when asked to turn on his side, sit up or raise his arms. *He can still follow orders*, I thought, smiling wryly.

On the fourth evening there was a change about the air in his room. I was apprehensive. Light shone from the overhead lamp as the room grew dismal. The gloom felt funereal. Anxiety tugged inside my chest. *What was that familiar odour?* It took a while to place, but then it came to me. *Mum smelt of it and now it's here too.* It was the sickly, sweet smell of death. Kneeling by his bedside, I held his old hand as his chest rattled and his lungs laboured for air, growing weaker, giving in.

Daylight stretched its fingers through a gap in the curtains, having long since chased night's darkness away. 'Not long now,' I whispered. Exhausted and emotional, I found myself suddenly startled by silence. I held my breath, straining to hear anything. Raising my eyes, I surveyed my grandad's face. He had gone.

Whimpering and tearful, I cradled his hand to my face. For minutes all was quiet until, without warning, came a horrifying gasp for air. My grandad's neck and head reached back into the pillow and his mouth opened. My heart beat out of its chest. I felt confusion and panic. *Is he alive?* I felt embarrassed that I'd been crying. *What if he knew you thought he was dead?* Holding my breath again I waited for him to exhale . . . it didn't come.

Only moments later, the clatter of the door handle pushing open resounded in my ears and two members of staff bustled in.

'Is it okay to get your grandad's sheets changed now?'

'No!' came my crumbling reply, 'it's not okay. It's too late.'

Early February found me standing at my grandfather's graveside, chilly and dejected as his coffin was lowered into the ground. All the people who had played their part in putting me on the planet were gone. I felt lost in the world; fearful and undone, entrenched in insecurity, totally and utterly alone. I wondered what the point of life was when it seemed so loaded with misery.

Words my grandad had once written to me in a letter, when I'd left home for the first time, echoed in my head, *We must all learn the hard lesson that the clock cannot be turned back. Once a path has been chosen, we've got to follow it, even although the going is rough at times. But I know you are tough enough and brave enough to do just that.*

I felt neither tough nor brave. I was angry and embittered. The past could not be altered. I would never again see either my grandparents or my mother, and I could not think of them in the past because the love I felt for them was with me in the present. I would not detach myself from the memories of how they cared for me as their granddaughter and daughter. It was impossible to reconcile life with death! Grief was so hideously, fucking lonely.

The only thing that kept me going was love for my sons. And that gave me the strength to limp on, albeit emotionally battered and bruised, into the future.

I searched the wintry skies for signs of the rescue helicopter. My ears strained against the occasional gusts of wind for the sound of its engine and blades. We'd been waiting an hour and twenty minutes, but it felt an eternity. And then I spotted a small, dark dot in my line of vision, but, with growing dismay, I watched as it circled distantly a few times then left. Paranoia set in. My children would finish their day at school soon and I wouldn't be home in time for them. I needed to get hold of the school and Leon's gran.

'I just spoke to the police again. They've confirmed Mountain Rescue is on the way. Ten more minutes, Sarah. Hang on in there,' Ollie comforted. I was cold in my awkward position, but heartened by the prospect of imminent rescue.

'If this had happened somewhere that doesn't have Mountain Rescue I'd be screwed. I'd have to try and drag myself back to the car on my elbows,' I said.

'I'd leave you. I wouldn't be able to stand listening to you saying how raging you are at yourself!' Ollie joked.

Suddenly the helicopter appeared over the mountain, its powerful blades whirring. It flew overhead, its pilot assessing the geography, while two figures at its open door, dressed in khaki clothing, gesticulated that the helicopter was going to fly around. Watching as it disappeared behind the curve of the mountain, I now felt a sense of urgency, I needed out of this remote place. Once more the helicopter rose into view then positioned its bulky metallic body directly above, rupturing the airflow and causing spindrift to thrust icy particles into our faces. I felt like I was going to slide again and tensed every muscle until my rescuer was winched down. Unclipping himself, he asked my name, age and what I'd hurt before strapping up my useless appendage and tying my good leg onto the splint too. 'We're ready to take you up. Keep your arms down and bend your knees like you're in a sitting position.' I closed my eyes as I was pulled high above the ground, but opened them when the downdraft from the helicopter's blades caused me to spin on the cable. I was frightened my splinted leg was going to thwack off the opening into the cabin.

Once I'd been safely hauled into the far corner, I thought about Ollie. I felt bad that we'd driven all this way and didn't even summit the mountains, that he'd had to hang around in the cold waiting for the rescue team and that now he had to do that long walk back to the car with my backpack as well as his own. In a way I hoped my ankle was broken so that my guilt was justified on account of both Ollie and the Mountain Rescue service – who had scrambled not only the aircrew, but also a team of sixteen who had been making their way to me by road. I'd put a lot of people out. An ambulance was waiting to transfer me to a hospital in Fort William, and as soon as I was there I asked to use a phone. My mind at rest that the boys would be fine, I was able to let the staff get on with their job. Medics crowded around.

'I'm going to need to take your boot off,' a nurse said apologetically.

'Please give me drugs before you take it off . . . *please!*' I begged her, with an eyeball-twisting wince.

'I'm sorry,' she said, shaking her head.

Turning my head, I closed my eyes and gripped the doctor's arm and bedrail as the boot was pulled. An X-ray confirmed what had been obvious: my ankle was broken. Back at the cubicle the nurse stripped me of my damp clothing.

'I didn't expect that!' she said, laughing.

'Is that how you hillwalkers dress these days?' asked the surprised doctor as he checked me out in my sparkly silver sequinned mini-dress.

'My Munro tally would have been 150 today. This was my outfit for the summit photo,' I explained.

'I'll take your photo for you now if you like?' said the smiling nurse.

'Can you wait till Ollie gets here with my afro wig? It's in my backpack,' I answered as a junior doctor fidgeted with a cannula, trying to insert it into my frozen, contracted vein. The staff were laughing. But I was now groaning as the anti-sickness fluid went in, ripping into my veins like a cat's claw.

'Don't worry,' the first doctor said, 'you're about to get the good stuff.'

'*Wooow!*' I purred in my silver dress as the morphine took effect, but despite the drug the doctor's several attempts at manipulating my bones back into place were still painful. I was at the hospital for over two hours before Ollie arrived, and four hours before they discharged me, telling me that I'd need to go home and attend hospital in Inverness the following day. My ankle was going to need surgery.

Ollie drove me back to Nairn.

'How are you going to get up four flights of stairs?' he asked. 'Do you want me to support you so you can hop?'

'I think it'd be less traumatic for my ankle if I shuffle up the steps on my butt, but thanks for the offer. And you don't need to hang about waiting for me to get to the top, I'll be fine,' I assured him: I'd wasted enough of his time.

'Okay. Well, if you're sure? I'll get off. Take care,' he said. And with that he left.

I hadn't shed a single tear all day – I'd sworn a lot but hadn't cried, until now. The exertion of getting up each dusty, dirty step of the communal stairwell was too much and I sobbed bitterly. A combination of the drugs and pain, frustration at how unnecessary the accident was and the question of how I was going to manage was overwhelming.

But although it all seemed so bleak, the accident was like the squeeze of a gun's trigger, and I was about to embark on a journey out of the blackness.

STEPS IN THE SUNSHINE

'Come, fill the Cup, and in the fire of Spring
Your Winter-garment of Repentance fling:
The Bird of Time has but a little way
To flutter — and the Bird is on the Wing.'

The Rubaiyat *of Omar Khayyam, VII*

CHAPTER FIFTEEN

One Thing Leads to Something Else

T he day after my accident, I asked my friend Paul to take me to hospital. I'd met him several years earlier when I was still with Sam. I'd needed to arrange some cosmetic repairs to the flat's interior, damaged by the leaking roof, and Sam had noticed him carrying out some work on the property next door. Paul agreed to come to the flat early evening and work till nine o'clock most nights, weekends too. He put on new skirting boards and facings, and I would sand, stain and oil them. He replastered and taped walls and ceilings for me to paint. He worked hard and I liked to watch. I liked how he wasn't full of typical male bravado; I liked the look on his face as he scribbled measurements and worked out sizes. He was competent, hard-working and honest, but best of all he spoke kindly and was nice to me. The worse things had become between Sam and me, the more I looked forward to times when I'd see Paul.

We'd stayed in touch over the years – whenever I needed a hand, whether with a bit of carpentry or tinkering with my car, it was him I turned to. And he always made himself available to me. So when I called him after my accident, he said he was happy to help.

For the first couple of weeks after surgery I was doped up on industrial-strength painkillers, and by mid February I felt toxic. All the while Paul had popped in and out to make sure I had what I needed, and that the boys were okay. One of my neighbours, who'd heard about my accident, also visited the flat, bringing us home-cooked meals; she even insisted on washing dishes and tidying up the kitchen more than once. I was bowled over by the kindness and generosity of this woman, who had been a total stranger before this. I found her motherly presence comforting, and her help invaluable; I was so grateful for her visits.

Fed up with taking pills, I reduced my dose. Continuous fatigue eased off and I soon realised that the good thing about being laid up meant there was plenty of time for reflection.

I took stock of my life, of the things that were making me unhappy, and the things I had the power to change, and the most obvious one was my career. After years of trying, I had to admit that teaching just wasn't for me. So I was going to forget it and return to my painting. I felt guilty for abandoning the path Mum would have picked for me; in some ways, even though she had been gone so long, I still sought her approval, but my time on the mountains had given me more confidence in myself and I was ready to cast aside idealised memories and choose a way that was going to make me, and therefore my children, happier.

Paul made me a huge easel and I was fired with enthusiasm. He'd also made other contraptions for keeping my leg raised at a comfortable angle on the sofa and the bed. I was coming to rely on him more and more, not just because he was helpful, but because he was patient and kind. It had only been a couple of years since I'd separated from Sam, but I began to muse what it might be like to be Paul's girlfriend.

When the boys were at school I continued my reading. I re-read my art school 'bible', E. H. Gombrich's *The Story of Art*. I read the biography of the Mexican artist Frida Kahlo, and then I flicked through *501 Great Artists* and was drawn to the image *Baby Giant*. The artist, Leonora Carrington, based her artworks on Aztec myth and mysticism. Before my accident I'd done a painting influenced by my own travels through Peru. These women inspired me to learn more about Latin American mythology. The reading I'd done supported my gut instinct. I was going back to my art, a world where I knew I belonged.

At last I was beginning to accept myself for who I was and not who I thought I should be.

Pondering what I might like to paint, I came across *The Origin of the Milky Way* by the Venetian artist Tintoretto and decided to make a colourful reproduction, to scale. The painting reminded me of my interest in Greek mythology, the universe, the stars from which we all come and nature itself. I looked out a varied selection of reading material to digest during long hours of incapacitation on the sofa – from *Granite and Grit* by R. Turnbull and *The Greek Myths* by Robert Graves to the *Children's Encyclopaedia of World Religion*. I find religion fascinating. Within its different branches there is such a rich diversity of practices and rites, yet commonalities also exist between different world religions and ancient myths. I felt excited by the possibility of working on a body of paintings, drawing from the theme of religious creation stories.

It was while I was carrying out more in-depth research on Hinduism that I had my next brainwave. *I should go to the Himalayas!* Excitement about an overseas trip grew; it would be ideal, combining a study trip with the enjoyment of mountains! And while it was not my initial reason for going, it did not escape my memory that this was where Gerry had died. I could visit his final resting place, and something about that felt like a fitting tribute to the man who had had such a profound impact on my life.

By early March I was able to get out on crutches. It was great to be more mobile again; I could sit properly and walk about the flat and I got to work on my new paintings. I even managed a couple of nights out when Paul drove me to and from Inverness to attend evening lectures by the climbers Stephen Venables and Simon Yates. Captivated by the former's description of his Himalayan expedition, I bought his book *A Slender Thread*, which I positively devoured and which revived my lust for a return to the hills.

One afternoon, as I rested on the sofa, I gazed at a painting Gerry had sent to my mum from Kathmandu. I'd never been fond of it, but I'd kept it as it had been special to her and that made it special to me. I looked at the multi-peaked, icy mountain against a lime-green wash and powder-blue sky. I could appreciate the artist's faithful rendition of the soaring bird of prey, and I pondered the painting's two signatures, R. L. Fleming and H. Poudyal.

Fleming was leader of the 1975 expedition and I was sure I remembered my mum telling me that it was a friend of Gerry's who had painted the picture.

On top of the wardrobe in my bedroom was a small, sturdy black case that had belonged to my mum. Retrieving the dusty case from its time-honoured post, I unclicked its silver clasps. Immediately the nostalgic and familiar scent of old paper wafted up. Once upon a time all Mum's secret stuff had been kept in here – private letters and photos. Before she died she had thrown out most of its contents but a few items survived: airmail letters from Gerry, a slightly out-of-focus Polaroid (the only picture of the pair together), photographs of him on expedition and, the item I was after, the bottle-green notebook detailing his Himalayan climbing exploits.

I read about climbs Gerry made to the Atlas Mountains, Morocco, to Tirich Mir in the Hindu Kush range of north-west Pakistan and to Indrasan in the Himachal Pradesh. But it was the 1970 Annapurna expedition in Nepal that made me feel most proud of his achievements. Annapurna is the tenth-highest mountain in the world; Gerry's ascent of it was a first for a British expedition team, and only the second in the mountain's history. (The first ascent of its north face – and in fact the first ascent of a mountain higher than 8,000 metres – had been made by the French mountaineers Maurice Herzog and Louis Lachenal twenty years earlier, in 1950.) But the success of Gerry's climb to the 8,090m peak was overshadowed by the first ascent of the mountain's steeper and more dangerous south face, just one week later, by two members of a team led by Chris Bonington.

Digging around inside the black case, I found the letters Gerry had sent to my mum, and also a Worcestershire and Sherwood Foresters Regimental Journal. Flicking through it, I stopped at a page that showed Gerry's face smiling back at me in black and white. Sadness that I'd been robbed of him as a father seeped back in.

The article reported on the accident in the Nepalese Himalayas that killed him; about how it was thought that Gerry and his climbing partner were hit and swept off Nuptse's south face by a heavy rockfall and that it was too dangerous for their bodies to be recovered by other expedition members. I learnt that he was the most distinguished mountaineer ever to have served in his regiment; the Colonel-in-Chief, Princess Anne, had conveyed sympathies to my mother, but it was a quoted tribute by General Sir Gerald Lathbury that I read through twice: 'We first met in Gibraltar, where I was Governor, and he was serving with his regiment. I heard that among his many activities he was interested in birds, so I roped him in to help in the observations I was carrying out . . .'

A penny was dropping. My brain cells were sparking like the friction between flint and stone. Excitedly I returned to Gerry's journal and scanned through the first and then second entry. His knowledge and understanding of birds – the feathered variety, as he had joked in one of his letters to Mum – was impressive, but more importantly his words, fluttering through the grey matter of my mind, had metamorphosed into understanding. It was as if I was stepping out into the glaring-bright light of day after spending almost fifteen years locked in darkness. I'd wanted to read about his mountain expeditions because I was interested in pursuing my own adventure, but his stories were the key to my liberation.

This was my eureka moment.

I'd often wondered where my mother's interest in ornithology had come from. Now I knew! Gerry had died, but by keeping his letters, photographs and journal, by walking and by surrounding herself with all things birds – from the painting, cushion covers, to the tapestries she stitched, and even school projects – she was preserving his memory. And, of course, there was the bangle.

When Gerry died, Mum shut out the world; she talked to no one. Just like I did when she died. She pursued a career in teaching to keep her mind busy and block out the misery of loss – probably the reason why she'd advised me to choose a similar career. Gerry's interest in ornithology became hers. And her interest in nature continues through me . . . it all began to make sense.

The people we love are the blueprint for our lives. At long last it felt that not only was I beginning to know who my mother was, but who I was too.

I dug out old calendars from a drawer in the bureau. Mum had often written down notes or thoughts on them and I wondered if her words would take on new meaning, but as I flicked through each I noticed something else. Every 9 May – the date Gerry had died – was circled in pen. She had never spoken about missing him, at least not to me. And though she'd enjoyed a few years of happiness with Frank, I was moved by Mum's enduring love for Gerry: I realised how little I really knew about this man who, despite his absence, had continued to have such an impact on our lives. I wanted to find out more about him. And suddenly I had an idea, a way of gaining closure and finally laying my mother's memory to rest. After years of holding on to her ashes, uncertain what to do with them, I knew what I needed to do.

In life Mum had been denied a future with Gerry, but in death I could reunite them. I decided to take her remaining ashes to Nepal and the Himalayas.

CHAPTER SIXTEEN

Protecting Next of Kin

B y the autumn of 2012, and my ankle having survived its test run, I'd got back on track working my way through the Munros. In the past two years I had shared long mountain days with my friend Mel. We were first introduced to each other when I'd come home from Cyprus, but although we'd been in and out of each other's lives since then we hadn't been particularly close. One day, however, we bumped into each other on the street and while we were chatting the subject of hills came up. Realising we both enjoyed walking, we made a plan to go together, and from that moment a more affectionate and meaningful bond grew between us. And eventually we discovered we had a lot more in common than just a mutual passion for hillwalking. At about the age I had lost my mum she had become estranged from her parents, so in a way she understood how it felt to be separated from family.

The more walks we did, the deeper we delved in conversation, till it came to the point where I found myself trusting her and felt I could honestly open up to her. This had been a gigantic step, as I'd felt anxious that she might distance herself from my company. But when I told her of those bad times, when I had been so low

I'd felt like ending it all, and of how pointless life seemed, she surprised me by confessing that she too had felt these same things. I remembered something Mum once said about having at least one good friend, and though it had taken many years, I felt with a growing certainty that Mel, at last, was that person.

I was the most content I had been in over a decade. My work was fulfilling, I had my next big project to plan, my children seemed to be growing up happily. And then there was Paul.

Paul had started to accompany me onto the hills, too. The more time we spent together, the closer we got. Slowly but surely I was falling in love with him. I knew he'd harboured feelings for me for some time too, but I didn't want to tell him how I felt until I was absolutely certain. The relationship I'd had with Sam had been a disaster, I'd dived right in. I didn't want a repeat of that, so I needed to take my time and be sure I wasn't gravitating towards Paul's love just because it was there. We'd known each other well for several years and I didn't want to throw this valuable friendship away. And, importantly, I needed to know if my children would approve.

'You like Paul, don't you?' I'd asked Leon one day.

'Yes. I like him as your friend. But I don't want him to be your boyfriend.'

Surprised by his perspicacity, I asked, 'What makes you think I want him for a boyfriend?'

'I've seen the way he looks at you.'

'Why wouldn't you want him to be my boyfriend?'

'I like things the way they are. It would be different.' The shine of my happiness dulled.

'You don't have to worry,' I said quickly. 'We're only friends.'

'Yes, but one thing leads to another,' my precocious but intuitive younger son commented.

I'd already spent weeks agonising over whether or not I could trust my feelings and not screw things up, and now Leon's opinion gave me further pause. But Paul made me feel happier than I had in years and so, finally throwing caution to the wind, I gave in to my feelings. On New Year's Eve Paul and I took the plunge and became a couple. I decided to see how things went between us before telling my boys, though; while Marcus would be accepting I already knew how Leon would react, so I expected a challenge ahead. But, remembering my own experience of how I'd first reacted to Frank, and how much I had regretted that later, I had to trust that Leon would eventually come around to the idea of Paul and me as a couple.

At the start of 2013 I set about finding out what I could about Gerry and his final climb. I returned to the little black case. A photograph of the memorial cairn, with the towering south face of Nuptse behind, and an airmail letter from Jon Fleming, the expedition's leader, were all that I had to go on. But at the head of the letter Jon had written that he was then a member of the Parachute Regiment; with this snippet of information I sent an email to the Ministry of Defence asking for their help to locate Jon and anyone else who knew Gerry.

At this time I also searched online for treks through the Khumbu Himal and found the 'Three Peaks, Three Passes' organised by Jagged Globe. The acclimatisation programme they were offering was ideal and, importantly, the main trail to Everest Base Camp would pass close to the valley that would lead me to Nuptse. I contacted Uncle Jimmy to tell him my plan.

'I'm going to take Mum's ashes to Nepal, to scatter her with Gerry; what do you think?'

'I couldn't have thought of anything better, Sarah.' My uncle's words were endorsement enough.

Without further hesitation, I contacted Jagged Globe and booked my place on their 2014 trek. The ball was rolling. Two weeks and thirty-three emails later, I had established contact with Jon Fleming and Henry Day – Gerry's climbing partner on Annapurna. Everything was coming together.

Henry Day and I stayed in regular contact, and I was soon invited to meet him and his wife Sara. During May I spent a weekend at their Cambridge home, where I was welcomed warmly. While I was there, friends of Henry and Sara – John Peacock and his wife Sheila – arrived late on Saturday afternoon. I liked them immediately. They were both quite short in stature. John's white hair was smartly coiffed, his crinkly blue eyes shone with generosity, and his kindly manner reminded me so much of my grandad. There was a motherly presence about Sheila that I felt instantly, and I almost wanted to hug both of them there and then. John had been with Gerry on Nuptse. He knew of my visit and had brought slides to show me. The four made me feel as if I was family, like I'd come home for the weekend and that I belonged.

I had brought the green notebook, some letters, a few photos and the only surviving wedding invitation intimating the details of Mum and Gerry's marriage.

'I hadn't realised that the relationship between your mum and Gerry had got so far; in fact I had no idea that they were to be married at all, let alone so soon after Nuptse,' said Henry.

'Did you know about my mum's relationship with Gerry?' I asked John.

'It was only at Gerry's memorial service that I was first introduced to her,' he answered.

'I remember meeting your mum,' Sheila said. 'John and I weren't even married at the time so I felt quite honoured that I was asked to go to Gerry's memorial. Your mum attended the service with Major Ian Leigh, and afterwards we all stayed overnight at John's sister's house. I told your mum that I'd met Gerry just the once, the night before he and John left for the Nuptse expedition. I'd been planning a cosy night for just myself and John at the opera to see *Cavalleria rusticana*, but John had asked if Gerry could go along too. It was the first opera Gerry had ever been to. Your mum told me that he had written to her, telling her all about it and that it had made a big impression on him. I was so happy to have given him that experience.'

I liked to hear Mum being talked about in conversation, but it struck me as more than a little odd that neither John nor Henry was privy to my mum and Gerry's wedding plans. The three men were good friends, so what was it with the secrecy? A host of nasties started whirling around my head as I puzzled over why Gerry had been a dark horse. I wanted to know why he'd kept the news of his marriage quiet – I was suddenly paranoid it had been because of me, because he was ashamed of Mum having an illegitimate child – but neither John nor Henry could tell me.

After the delicious dinner that Sara had cooked for us, Henry, Sheila and I settled down to listen to John recount with slides the expedition's journey to Nepal, the days preceding the tragedy on Nuptse, and the terrible unfolding of the accident that led to Gerry's death. I was sitting next to Sheila, and she asked me:

'Why now, after all these years?'

Her directness caught me off guard, but I tried to explain.

'Because I have been so utterly miserable since Mum died. I don't really feel I've ever got over it, in a way. Then I discovered Gerry's journal. I read it and suddenly realised how little I really knew about him, about them. He was a great love of my mum's life. Now I need to know more about the kind of man he was and the relationship they had.'

Sheila nodded.

Whisky's nostalgic aroma scented the room as Sara brought in a dram for Henry and John. I let its warm memories of Christmases past fill my lungs as John began his story. He spoke and we listened without interruption.

'Directed right around the airfield at Heathrow, five of us arrived at a discreet little lounge, out of sight of the public view, and waited for the Comet to appear. We were the advance party on our way to Nepal and scheduled to fly, hitch-hiking by courtesy of the RAF, as supernumeraries with HRH Prince Charles, on his way to represent Her Majesty, his mother, at the Coronation of King Birendra in Kathmandu. HRH was our Expedition Patron and seemed more than happy to help. The few days we spent in Kathmandu were fascinating, as was the coronation procession itself. But we left all that behind and suddenly found ourselves camped above a native village, not a light in sight, in stark contrast with the city still celebrating miles behind us.

'Ahead lay nearly two weeks of steady tramping, across the grain of the country, over and down ridge after ridge. Crops in the valleys, and rhododendrons scarlet on the hillsides, formed an ever-changing backdrop to the human activities. Gerry was in seventh heaven as he could really indulge his interest in birds. He would set off every morning a good two hours ahead of the rest of us so he had time to study them. Long before we reached Namche Bazaar, the main Sherpa centre, he had spotted and identified more than 300 different indigenous species. Even so, it was not until we had established our base camp, close to the Nuptse Glacier, that he finally caught sight of the huge Himalayan vulture that so fascinated him, the lammergeier. It has an enormous two-and-a-half-metre wingspan; it dwarfs all other species.

'What happened next remains a mystery to us all. Two days earlier we'd last seen Gerry and Richard, his climbing partner, around mid-morning, climbing steadily towards the top of the couloir, the steep ravine, and the start of the relatively short rocky ridge leading to the summit. So we watched and waited, hoping against hope they were still climbing but somehow hidden from our view. But they seemed to have simply disappeared.

'The following morning, with no radio call from the summit or elsewhere, we were forced to accept the worst. We sent a signal via the Embassy in Kathmandu to the Royal Nepalese Army, and they immediately offered to send a helicopter to help search the following day. The Alouette helicopter whisked two of us up the glacier and into a huge amphitheatre of rock walls, to land on the ice just a few hundred yards below the crevasse between the glacier and the rock. Above reared a huge, shallow rock face, almost vertical in the lower hundred feet before leaning back at a slightly shallower angle towards the similarly steep mixed slopes above: an unremitting and more or less continuous line leading eventually to the final couloir and the route to the summit. Anything falling from the couloir would probably continue down this chute. Finally we discovered Richard's boot on the glacier surface some distance short of the bergschrund, confirming that we had come to the right place. A few more yards enabled us to peer over the edge to confirm our worst fears.

'Nigel and I found them, Gerry and Richard, lying quite close to each other on an icy shelf some 40 feet down. Below the shelf the crevasse continued into the depths. Both bodies were cocooned in coils of rope, suggesting that, whatever had caused their fall, they must have rolled for some distance down the steep slope of the snow-filled ravine.

'Some yards to the left there appeared to be a relatively straightforward means of climbing into the crevasse, on a level and connecting with the shelf on which Gerry and Richard lay. While one of us organised a belay, securing a rope to an anchor to enable us to get back up and out of the crevasse, the other set off to climb down and along but had barely started before Pierre, our French pilot, 'buzzed' us, the prearranged signal that he was running short of fuel. Scrambling quickly out onto the glacier surface, we made our way across to the aircraft and climbed aboard. Wasting no time, Pierre took off back to Base Camp, asking no questions: our nods and the looks on our faces were doubtless enough.

'With most of the expedition engaged well up the route, there were only a few people left at Base Camp. In any case, the trauma of our recent discovery perhaps obliterated all but the most significant details, including Pierre's gentle courtesy as he left us alone immediately after we landed, and again that same consideration as we made our farewells and very grateful thanks before he left to fly back to Kathmandu. For a little while I busied myself with routine things, trying the while to come to terms with events, before realising that Nigel was no longer in the camp.

'Even at 17,000 feet it was a very hot morning, but I found Nigel just a few hundred yards along the gently sloping valley leading to Pokalde. He was sitting on a boulder, his chin in his hands and obviously distressed. Neither of us spoke; there was no need. How do you reconcile such a perfect day in such magnificent surroundings with what we had both witnessed just a few hours earlier? Then a lammergeier appeared, almost it seemed from nowhere, to fly majestically past us on the same level and barely twenty yards away, its huge wings stretched out to bear it effortlessly past until, gently turning, it came back to us, a little higher now, only to continue its turn, complete the circle and commence another, higher still. We gazed, fascinated by this magnificent bird, as slowly it spiralled up and up and still up for minutes on end. Losing track of time, neither of us could follow it further as it grew smaller and ever smaller. One moment it was still there, the next it had simply disappeared into the heavens.

'We sat there, speechless. Both of us knew that Gerry had been more than enthusiastic about birds of all kinds; even more significant was the fact that he had said only a week earlier that the bird he most admired was the great bearded vulture, the lammergeier. He had added that, if there was such a thing as reincarnation, he would like to come back as, yes, a lammergeier.'

John retold the tale with composure and clarity, but now his voice wavered, overcome with emotion as he remembered the sadness – we all felt it. A heavy silence bore down on our small group as we sat around the open fire. Seeing slides of the journey that the expedition had taken gave me a good idea of what to expect on my trek the following year, but I couldn't shake off the concoction of distress, horror and anger as I stared at the final slide of Nuptse's forbidding and hostile south face. After Gerry and his climbing partner died, a second summit bid had been made. Two more men perished, this time lower down the mountain. It was only then that the pursuit of victory over Nuptse was abandoned.

'I have a painting at home that was done by the expedition's leader, Jon Fleming. It's of a bird of prey flying in front of a mountain,' I said, breaking the stony silence.

'How interesting, it would be fascinating to see it,' said Henry. When I showed him a photograph of the painting he exclaimed, 'That's Annapurna!'

'And the bird is undoubtedly a lammergeier,' John added. 'I remember Gerry talking about having met a father-and-son team in Kathmandu before the expedition set off for Nuptse. Yes, it's coming back to me now.' The surname Fleming was mere coincidence and the painting was not done, as I had previously assumed, by the expedition's leader. 'Gerry and I had supper with two delightful Americans – natural historians who were producing a definitive bird book on Nepal. Gerry had first met them in 1970 and had corresponded with them since; they had struck up a bond of friendship cemented by a mutual enthusiasm for ornithology. Gerry introduced the Flemings to me in February 1975. R. L. Fleming and his son of the same name lived and worked together in Nepal; their base was in Kathmandu.'

After a little further research on my part I learnt that Robert Fleming had been studying birds for twenty-five years and, at the time of his meeting Gerry, he was in the process of having a publication entitled *Birds of Nepal* put into print. He himself was also the subject of a book, *The Fabulous Flemings of Kathmandu*, which told the story of how he founded the first modern hospital in Nepal in 1956. Hem Poudyal, the second signature on the painting, was the artist; he had devoted three years to Robert Fleming's project, persevering with the meticulous depiction of approximately 800 species of birds. Gerry had commissioned the painting, now in my possession, and had instructed that on completion it be sent to my mother.

Discovering its story gave me a new sense of appreciation for the painting. It was no longer some kind of bird against a gaudy-coloured background; it was the magnificent lammergeier flying triumphantly before Gerry's prized and conquered Annapurna.

Everyone went to bed. I sent a text to Paul, sharing my day's news before switching off my phone. I wished I could switch off the thoughts in my head too, but as I lay there I couldn't seem to stop my mind from returning to the question of why Gerry had kept quiet about marrying Mum.

After breakfast Sara and Henry showed Sheila around the garden, which gave John and me the opportunity to talk some more about Gerry.

'How do you think they came to fall?' I asked.

'That will always remain a mystery. We can never know, but Gerry died doing something he loved.'

'He loved my mum too though.' I told John about my mum dying and about how she had asked for the bangle. Tears flowed from my eyes as I opened up. 'I'm sorry for crying.'

'Crying is nothing to be sorry for. It means you have been loved and you love,' John said gently. Pulling myself together, we went outside to take a photograph of us all before John and Sheila left for home.

Sara and Henry went to church, leaving me to root through a couple of boxes of papers and photographs that Henry had dug out for me – I wasn't looking for anything in particular, but perhaps there might be something that would tell me more about Gerry. It felt a nice kind of weird being left in their house on my own; a privilege to be trusted because, up till now, I had been a perfect stranger.

There was such a lot to sift through, many duplicates and endless lists of equipment. Scanning over a couple of pages from the expedition newsletter, I saw it contained information that could be useful to photocopy in preparation for my own trek the following year – stuff like the types of flora and fauna that are found locally, species of birds and names of settlements.

An airmail letter from Jon Fleming to Henry caught my eye. It had been sent from Nuptse Base Camp and simply correlated with everything else I'd heard and read, while also expressing condolences and a request not to intimate its contents to the press – 'to protect the feelings of next of kins'. I continued to flick through papers such as a copy of the Memorial Service Distribution List, which named all the relatives and military personnel who attended it at Worcester Cathedral. There was a postcard of Mount Ama Dablam and, turning it over, I instantly recognised Gerry's handwriting.

Camp II – 18,000 feet 22 April

Dear Sara and Henry,

Many thanks for your letter – most welcome. First and foremost, delighted to hear of Katherine's arrival; my congratulations to you both – great news! Yes, despite too many godchildren already, I am most happy to accept but June may be a v difficult month for me. Apparently we have now reached the most difficult part of the climb. Expedition is far too large as I mentioned to you before I left UK. I hope your Everest Log Plan reduces members!

As ever, Gerry

Weird! Of course June would be a bit tricky for him – he was getting married to my mother! Confusion bubbled again. Why was their marriage such a big secret? With not much time left available before my late-afternoon flight I had to be swift with my photocopying. I'd tidied up by the time Sara and Henry returned and was making some last copies in Henry's office when he came in and rummaged around in a cupboard. 'Here, I'll loan you my

Royal Geographic Map of the Everest Region. It should come in handy, you'll be able to gauge the route your trek will take in more detail – always better to know where you are going even if you don't know what you will encounter on the way.' I thanked him.

I had gone to Cambridge hoping to learn more about the man my mum loved, the man who would have brought me up and, according to my Aunt Penny, had vowed to look after me and love me like I was his very own. But while I took away some answers, I had also found more questions.

CHAPTER SEVENTEEN

History Repeats Itself

Fisherfield, July 2013

July 2013 was hot. The group of Fisherfield Munros, located in Wester Ross, were fairly remote, but I'd been keen to go camping there for some time. Heaving on 40lb rucksacks, Paul and I set off along Loch Maree. It was afternoon; the dry heat was already intense and as wearing as the clegs – pellet-shaped flying insects whose vicious bites kept drawing blood from the bare skin of my arms and legs. They were driving me nuts. We beat our way through high sections of tall bracken on the narrow trail, trying not to trip over protruding rocks and tree roots. It took us an hour before we reached a bridge that signalled the long haul up Gleann Bianasdail. A series of stunning waterfalls had carved the rock into square, flat platforms, and water cascaded over the edges like the veils of a thousand brides.

Deep into the glen we were hemmed in by the secluded valley walls, and, struggling with the weight of our heavy packs, our march had slowed to a plod as we baked in the heat. Loch Fada finally came into view, but any hopes that we were nearly there were seriously misjudged. Still, it was only three and a half hours after leaving the car at Incheril when I finally plonked my backpack down on the shingle beach at the loch's head. It didn't rest there long. There was barely enough time to appreciate the beauty before it was spoilt by the entire Fisherfield contingent of clegs and midges on their search-and-destroy mission; the place was alive with them, and I danced and swatted in an attempt to fend them off. Throwing the tent up at breakneck speed, we flung our packs, and ourselves, into the insect-free zone.

At six o'clock we left the sanctuary of the tent for our evening hike up to the summits of A' Mhaighdean and Ruadh Stac Mor, hoping that our winged foes were in abeyance. We trudged along over uneven, rough and boggy terrain, the heathers scratching around our ankles. While it was still light I took bearings from landmarks we picked out – the nipple on top of a hillock, the right-hand side of two rounded lumps on higher ground, and so on. I was pretty good at this map-reading stuff now. Slioch was reflected in the loch, and as we climbed higher more Torridonian giants soared into view. Day was fading. Quietness instilled a perfect peace and I paused to watch two young deer silhouetted on the ridgeline. Absorbed by the task of climbing uphill over the rough heathers, I got quite a fright when the head of a stranger, popping up over the top of a tent, suddenly came to view. I was disappointed that we didn't have the peak to ourselves so Paul and I pressed on towards the second Munro.

As we walked along the ridge the sun's rays washed the surrounding land and mountains in glorious colour. Dubh Loch and Fionn Loch glittered like swathes of silver ribbon far below. Ahead the red-sandstone cliffs of Ruadh Stac Mor were set aglow in a salmon pink. In the near distance An Teallach resembled a fortress, with beetling crags and a ragged ridge that punctured the skyline like scores of broken glass bottles. Atmospheric conditions created blocks of colour that made the complex architecture of the mountain scenery look almost two-dimensional. The night was intoxicating, and I was definitely in love.

Though we had been discreet, Paul and I couldn't hide our relationship from my children for ever. As expected, my youngest son hadn't taken the news so well.

'You said you wouldn't have him for a boyfriend. You lied to me!' he cried. His distress struck a chord. I'd put off telling my boys about the relationship because I'd wanted them to get used to having Paul around, to get to know and like him more and to protect their feelings – probably the same reasons why my mother had kept quiet about Frank; she had wanted me to accept him in my own time.

'Leon, I'm sorry,' I'd said gently, 'things changed.'

'Why couldn't you just stay friends?'

'I suppose because we spent more time together. I trust him. He has shown us all kindness and has given all of us help whenever we've needed it – how many times has he come to catch spiders?' I asked. But my attempt to raise a smile was met with a scowl. I realised that whether I'd been honest about Paul or not, the outcome remained the same. Just as I had vied for my mother's attention, my son sought mine. It seemed I couldn't stop history repeating itself.

The trail began to thread its way up through cliffs, steeply in places, over loose sandstone screes. I enjoyed the easy scrambling to reach the second summit. I pulled on my down jacket, yanked on some leggings and took the squashed roll and can of Jack Daniels from my backpack. As I sat on a summit rock, warm air caressed my face and dusky pinks and mellowing violets coloured the sky, casting warmth onto the mountains. I found it hard to believe that these towering bastions, with their shattered spires and jaggy ridges like filed teeth, could be such hostile environments and the takers of life. Soaking in the beauty, I thought about Gerry, Mum, my grandparents and my children. And I thought about the future. Paul and I talked.

'I know things are a bit tricky with Leon, but if we love each other enough we can ride the storm, can't we?' I said.

'Sarah, I love you and I always will. I waited so long for you, I'm not going to stop now.' Paul's answer was everything I needed to know.

'So, what do you think about me going to Nepal? Will you miss me?'

'Yeah, course I'll miss you. But it's a big deal for you and it's what you need to do, isn't it? Anyway, you'll only be away for a month.'

'Well. I was wondering if maybe you would want to come with me. What do you think?'

'Do you want me to?' he asked with surprise.

I could tell he was touched that I'd asked. That was what I also loved about him; he was so unassuming. We toasted our celebration with a tinny clunk of our Jack Daniels and watched the sun as it set. For the first time in my life I hadn't rushed in, and, in spite of all my imperfections, I knew I was truly loved.

At ten-thirty it was time to descend. Returning in the dark was in some ways easier than walking during daylight. We had to rely on the bearing I took and walk on it faithfully, whereas in daylight, although I use my map and compass, I'm also observing the lie of the land, trying to pick out an easier line. Of course night walking was not without its pitfalls. All was going well until I lost my left and then my right foot into ankle-deep bog, but silvery moonlight reflecting in a small lochan nearby lifted my spirits and that, combined with our earlier conversation, made the night feel enchanting as we squelched blindly on. I tried to avoid further soakings as blisters gnawed, my feet rubbing in wet socks against my boots. But no amount of discomfort could spoil my contented mood. At two in the morning we were back in the tent eating the last of our pasta, and more than ready for sleep.

Paul and I woke up gulping for air. Though it was only seven in the morning the sun's heat was already burning through the thin nylon tent fabric. It was suffocating, but I didn't dare unzip the flap when I saw the tens of thousands of black, pinhead-sized bodies splattered against the green outer shell. Desperate for air, I opened the inner flap, squashing my mouth and nose against the midge net. A few gentle wafts of air off the loch gave momentary relief, but the stifling heat became torturous. Packing up swiftly, we braced ourselves for the apocalyptic attack as we emerged from the tent . . . and right on cue the dancing and swatting routine began. A calm scene by comparison,

Slioch was mirrored in minute detail in Loch Fada as waters lapped idly against the shingle with neither a whisper of wind nor a cloud in the sky.

We left the tent and made our way across boggy ground and scratchy shrubs. Jumping over squelchy, dark-brown hag onto dried yellow sprigs of grasses, we made a direct line to the south ridge of our first Munro. Once we gained its lower section we had to pick a way across an expanse of glacially exposed flat rock. Too much sun, tiredness and not having eaten was making me feel sick and, remembering my previous experience, I had to stop and force some food down. After ten minutes we pressed on slowly, conserving energy – trying not to perspire too much. My feet, in their wet accommodation, were already in pain.

A footpath took us the rest of the way to the summit and we ate an early lunch in what little shade there was. My bread was difficult to swallow. It felt dry and rough as it passed slowly down my gullet. It was only eleven and the worst of the heat was to come, but superb views to An Teallach and the full Fisherfield horseshoe compensated for my minor physical difficulties. And because John Peacock had told me that these mountains were a favourite haunt of Gerry's, they held more meaning for me.

As Paul and I walked down the wide, grassy ridge we saw folk camped out on the col below. More people were making their way up lower slopes from Loch Fada. The hills were busy.

'John Peacock told me that back in the 1950s his friend Mike O'Hara was the first man to have completed the three peaks, Ben Nevis, Scafell Pike and Snowdon, in under twenty-four hours. And apparently Mike loved climbing here too. There were no paths or Munro-baggers back then,' I continued. 'It must have been exciting to explore these hills; that's real adventure, isn't it?'

'Yeah, it's too easy today. There's all those online sites with their free route descriptions and maps to download,' Paul said.

'I wish I'd been an explorer.'

'Being with you *is* a daily adventure. I doubt I could take much more excitement,' Paul joked, and I gave him a shove, pretending to be put out. I was so happy. Respite from the sun's infernal blaze as we walked in the shadow of Meall Garbh increased my pleasure, and as luck would have it a nice, fat cloud lazily pulled across the sky, blocking those violent rays for most of the battle up the ridge to our second summit of the day.

I felt like the little mermaid. My fiery feet were in tatters as I relieved them of their Gore-Tex prisons to totter across the sum-mit stones. My vest was soaked, so I peeled it off too and sat in my bra and skirt at the cairn. I eyed up Sgurr Ban. Our third peak lay just over one kilometre away.

'We're running low on everything, Sarah. There's hardly any water left and this heat's a killer. I know you won't want to, but I think we should abandon it,' Paul said.

It was hard to turn my back on that last summit.

'The hill isn't going anywhere. We can come back and do it another day. We've still gotta get down and dismantle the tent, and that's before the long walk out too. The boys have school tomorrow and you don't want to be too late to pick them up from their grandparents,' he added. Paul was right. I was all gung-ho and that's how accidents happen, and he was the voice of reason, a calming influence: he was the yin to my yang.

CHAPTER EIGHTEEN

Dark Horse

The Inaccessible Pinnacle, September 2013

Crepuscular light filtered through the sky at about quarter past seven as we sped along the road towards Skye. The Glen Shiel Mountains made a good barrier against the rising sun and created a stunning silhouette, but we were off to climb the hardest mountain summit to reach on the British Isles, the Inaccessible Pinnacle, or In Pinn. To tackle the In Pinn we had needed to learn some basic rock climbing, so we'd taken a weekend course near Betws-y-Coed. The same skills could have been taught closer to home, but because I'd discovered, through correspondence with another contact of Gerry's, that he had enjoyed climbing in Snowdonia I'd decided it was there that Paul, Marcus, Leon and I would take our instruction. We were kitted out with equipment – harnesses, climbing shoes and the like – then it was off to Plas y Brenin and the Pinnacles to be shown the basics of rock climbing. After a morning of instruction, learning how to tie on, make figure-of-eight knots, use safety anchors and abseil, we tackled a couple of climbs on a large slab of rock, whose cracks ran like tramlines in criss-cross patterns, at Little Tryfan. The day had been absorbing, but it was about to get more interesting. We were off to Llangollen, to meet Gerry's cousins, Rod and Jill.

Through initial contact with the Ministry of Defence my email address had finally trickled down the line to Rod Owens. I was ecstatic when he got in touch. Members of my family hadn't been able to shed light on why Gerry might not have broadcast his wedding plans, and it was still bothering me. Uncle David's impression at the time was that Gerry's parents had been unhappy about him marrying my mother because she had a child, and that they threatened to cut him off if he went ahead with the wedding. Aunt Penny, though, had told me that she didn't think Gerry's parents were alive. She thought that he had been brought up either by an aunt or by a foster mother. Uncle Jimmy knew no more than Uncle David. It was a muddle of information that made Gerry and his life an enigma. But now I was in a position to ask about family, and I had to hope that Rod would provide the answers I was looking for.

Arriving at the bistro in Llangollen ahead of Rod and Jill, we had time to order a drink. I felt nervous. There was no mistaking Rod when he walked in. His handsome, angular features resembled my own memories and the photos of Gerry. His eyes and smile were similar too. Both he and Jill were pleasant and easy company, but it transpired that Rod knew very little about Gerry himself, and Jill had never even met him!

'I'm afraid I know nothing of the relationship between your mother and my cousin,' he said.

Not even his family knew he was getting married! My heart sank to the pit of my stomach.

'What about his parents? Do you know anything about them?' I asked.

'His father was killed in action in North Africa when he was thirty-six. His grave is out there,' said Rod, sifting through photographs to show me a picture of the headstone. 'Gerry's mother, Edith, didn't cope with his death. She had a breakdown and was, unfortunately, institutionalised. Gerry, his two brothers and two sisters were split up and sent off to different people to be looked after, but the brothers then attended Duke of York's Military School, before Gerry then went on to Sandhurst. He kept contact with his two sisters, Jean and Bernice, possibly more than he did with the brothers.'

'Is anyone in touch with the brothers and sisters?'

'The older brother is dead, and the other brother lost touch with the family of his own volition. It would be impossible to track him down. I really don't know if anyone's in touch with the sisters, but I'll do my best to find out,' Rod said.

Three hours had been a long time for Marcus and Leon to sit quietly, but our evening had finally come to an end. Apart from one swift kick Leon had given his brother under the table that had gone unnoticed by all except me, the boys had been on their best behaviour and I was proud of them.

'Your boys are so well behaved, they're a credit to you,' Jill said, smiling at them.

Agreeing to send on copies of pictures, we said our goodbyes and promised to keep in touch. I felt we would, just as Gerry's old climbing partner Henry Day and I had maintained contact – we'd corresponded regularly since our first meeting and had arranged to see each other again, on the In Pinn on Skye.

On the second day of our weekend course in Wales we'd gone to the Moelwyns, sixteen miles from Betws-y-Coed. Slate mines lined each side of the road: blue slate was quarried on the right, purple on the left. We pulled in at an already busy car park and walked up a trail to cliffs where a couple of ropes were at work. A cold wind gusted. Our guide, Dave, led Leon and me on a route called 'Slick', while Marcus and Paul had started a few minutes ahead of us with their instructor. Leon climbed second and I followed behind. He made me feel warm-hearted as he called out words of encouragement. Sharing our struggles and achievements today was helping to build an even closer bond with him, bridging the gap that had opened up when I'd started seeing Paul. Reaching Dave, who had us secured by a sling around a tree, I saw Marcus ahead. His body was wedged, feet against one wall, back against the other, as he wriggled his way up a narrow chimney – a fissure in the rock.

'That looks tricky!' I exclaimed.

'You missed seeing Paul get up. It was a performance of brute force rather than technique!' said Dave, then, turning to Leon, asked, 'Shall we abseil back down from here? The chimney might be too difficult. What do you think?'

'I want to try it!' Leon exclaimed, not to be outdone by his older brother, as he scrabbled and struggled up the chimney. Seeing him succeed filled me with pride – and also gave me a nudge of confidence that I could do it too. After one final pitch – as the section of climb between two fixed points is known – we were at the top of the 100-metre crag.

Leon watched with Paul and Marcus as Dave and I climbed one more route. When the rope stopped sliding through my hands I knew that Dave was either putting in an anchor to make himself safe or there was a trickier section of rock to climb. I was tied onto Dave, but he had disappeared from view and the rope had almost paid out. It felt strange standing alone on the narrow, rocky shelf so high above ground. As my hands gripped the wall I wondered if this route might have been one that Gerry had done and I tried to imagine how it would have felt to be climbing with him.

'That's me!' Dave called, interrupting my thoughts. Up I went. 'That was fast!' he exclaimed, as my head appeared over the rock. At the top of the crag Dave showed me how to coil ropes correctly to carry them. 'You should be quite pleased with yourselves. Those climbs we did are classed as a very difficult and a severe 4a*.' I didn't really know what that meant, but if he was pleased then I was delighted.

With our rock-climbing weekend over, we had one more visit left to make before leaving Wales.

When I'd returned from the weekend in Cambridge with Henry and Sara I'd had mixed emotions but wasted no time in trying to find more contacts from Gerry's past. Determined that there was someone somewhere who knew of his relationship with my mother, I needed reassurance. If I was going to take her ashes all the way to Nepal then I had to be 100 per cent sure that Gerry had truly loved her too – there could be no doubt. I looked out letters from the little black case written to Mum by my grandfather, searching for any kind of clue at all. Though it felt like clutching at straws, it was, all the same, a comfort to read his words. Hearing Grandad's voice in my head as I read the letter, I did find something worth going on:

> *Mum told me you had got the photographs of Gerry, so Ian Leigh must have dropped them in. He got them from a Dr Jones in Canada, who was on the Annapurna expedition with Gerry. He had promised to send them to Ian a long time ago and when he finally did the other day he said he would send duplicates to you if Ian thought you might like them. Ian accepted on your behalf and in the meantime gave you his copies.*

I got in touch with Henry, hopeful that he might have contact details for the men mentioned in the letter. Ian Leigh had died some years ago, but Henry passed on an email address for Dr Jones. I'd assumed that the doctor lived in Canada so was surprised, after sharing my rock-climbing plans with him, when he invited me, Paul and the boys to come for dinner – he and his wife lived forty minutes away from Betws-y-Coed. As Dr Jones said, it was serendipity indeed.

Finding Dolfriog Lodge proved to be a task as tricky as our earlier climbs. We finally found the lodge, out in the sticks along more of the overgrown, single-track, twisting roads, hidden amid trees and luscious green foliage, built high on rock with a fast-flowing river below. The noise of the car in this remote place alerted Dr Jones and his wife to our arrival and they came out to greet us at the gate. Glenys was a character larger than life, and she bestowed a massive hug and kiss on each of us as her husband, David, after a warm handshake, ushered us into the house. While he tended to the roasting meat, Glenys regaled us with a little local history. The slow-cooked lamb in mint with new potatoes, carrots and broccoli was delicious. After dinner we at last got down to the business of Gerry.

'We first became acquainted on the Annapurna expedition, you see. We just clicked,' said David. 'Gerry and I had been close. I considered us to be good friends. We remained in regular contact after Annapurna . . .'

Glenys interjected, 'I was very fond of Gerry. He and all the Annapurna climbers came to visit us for a reunion. I remember him saying, "I don't know why I'm in the army, I'm a pacifist."' With that she erupted into laughter.

'So, did you know about my mum and Gerry?' I asked David.

'I'm afraid I had no knowledge of their engagement. I didn't even know there was a girl on the scene. But, you see, he was a very private person, a dark horse even among close friends. It was hard to know what went on in his mind.'

By now I was getting used to these kinds of comments. Digging out an old address book, he scribbled down details of two contacts.

'The address is for Cattie. She's the wife of Andy Anderson; sadly he died several years ago, but he was a great friend of Gerry's. I think Cattie will be the one most able to help you.'

'Gimme another jelly sweet,' I said. 'Your driving's making me feel sick.'

'Sorry, but you told Henry we'd meet him at the memorial hut at eight. We're running late,' Paul answered.

As the car took us over the brow of a hill and further into Glen Brittle, the Skye Cuillin ranged into view; on its tobacco-coloured cushion of empty moorland the ridge was a spiky crown in shadowy shades of blue and purple. Early-morning cloud wrapped around the ancient volcano's base like a fine silk scarf. Henry greeted us at the memorial hut and then, laden with backpacks and ropes, we set off on the trail. I'd only been here once before, but everything was as I recalled it: the 25-metre-high Eas Mor waterfall tumbling into the tree-filled gorge, the stony terrain and the sense of high adventure.

Our route began on an obvious man-made track before it became rockier. There were plenty of cairns, which took a devious line beneath the crags of Sgurr Dearg. We could have followed these up into a gully, which would have put us on the ridge, but we went left onto screes that led to a gap in the line north of Sgurr Dearg. Paul topped out first.

'Well, there it is,' he said. His tone and the look on his face did not impart a sense of joy.

I arrived at his side. 'Ahhh,' I said, in serious contemplation.

'Mmm . . . okay,' said Henry, as he appeared behind us.

We dropped our kit and sat for a few minutes to enjoy views of the ridge extending east and west, and to Rum, one of the small isles of the Inner Hebrides, before Henry handed us a harness each. We descended slabby rock to the base of the In Pinn. We spotted someone on nearby Sgurr Mhic Choinnich, and closer still a woman in shorts and a vest, blonde hair scraped back in a ponytail;

she was alone and moving fast. As I waited to climb I looked up at the blue sky. A raven, dark as night, with wings at full span circled up from behind the rock. Then another raven appeared, and another. I was watching their theatrical performance with fascination when into view came a whopping wingspan. Henry reckoned it was an immature golden eagle to whom the ravens were giving chase.

Henry started up the east ridge of the Pinn, a moderate rock climb but incredibly exposed: a foot wide with 'an overhanging and infinite drop on one side, and steeper and further on the other', as one early mountaineer had described it. The rock climbing in Wales stood us in good stead for this.

'Safe,' Henry called, as he made the first of two pitches. I took him off belay and he pulled in the rope.

'That's me,' cried Paul.

'Climb!' Henry shouted down to me.

Off I went. Busy concentrating on finding foot- and hand-holds, I didn't even think to look down. I was fine, though taking my time, when the lone, blonde-haired woman scrambled quickly up past me, unroped! I admired, and slightly envied, her bold and confident attitude. Parts of the rock felt smooth under my hands and fingers, no doubt worn down over the passage of time by countless climbers and Munroists. Making sure I had three points of contact, I pulled myself up, momentarily imagining what it might be like to come off and how unpleasant it would be to pendulum out and smash into solid rock, but I shook the thought from my mind. Before long I reached Henry and was soon perched behind him, safely clipped into the sling.

The second pitch was initially steep but easy, and the abseil off was fun. Gathering in the rope, we returned to our earlier perch on high rock to eat lunch and watched as two guys began what we had just completed.

I wished that my confidence in Gerry was as solid as the rock we'd been climbing over. The mystery surrounding his relationship with Mum remained unresolved, but having met his friends, in particular the cousins, made him feel less of a ghost, and there were new leads.

I wasn't about to give up on anything.

CHAPTER NINETEEN

Walking on Air

Aonach Mor and Aonach Beag – the Big Ridge
and the Little Ridge, April 2014

S trong winds and blizzard conditions across the Scottish Highlands put paid to regular hillwalking over the winter months. By January I missed being on the mountains and was beginning to fret that there were only a few months left to get into good condition for the high-altitude trek in Nepal, but I built up my stamina by weight-training and running ten kilometres every day, and Paul just carried on working. He was fit anyway, going up and down ladders, digging like a slave and lifting heavy blocks. What bothered me more than our physical health was that I still hadn't found any of Gerry's friends who knew he had planned to be married. If I could hear what I wanted from just one person I'd feel vindicated in taking Mum's ashes to him.

I'd written to Cattie Anderson but, having heard nothing back, I'd given up on that lead. But then one day, in March, a reply arrived in the post. My heart sank at first, scanning the first three paragraphs, which seemed to suggest I'd drawn another blank, but I soon discovered how wrong I was as I read on:

Andy left the Army in 1973 or 74 – he was scared they were going to send him to Ireland – but he continued to work as a civilian instructor and was expecting to be on the team for Everest in 1976. In 1975 he was appointed as an instructor at Glenmore Lodge, and I think that this is why he didn't go to Nuptse. As it happened, he broke his leg quite seriously in a skiing accident and spent some time in Raigmore hospital. It was while he was there that he heard of Gerry's death. Sadly, a few days after that he received a letter from Gerry asking him to be best man at his wedding – that really cut him up.

The words in Cattie's letter were exactly I had been looking for. Clearly, Andy and Gerry had been close and, whatever secrecy Gerry had applied elsewhere to his plans, he had made his intentions crystal clear to Andy. Elated with the news, I cast aside doubt. I felt I was walking on air.

I'd also met up again with John and Sheila, as John had brought the Nuptse expedition map to show me. We compared his original route to the one I would be making with Jagged Globe.

'Can you show me where to find the memorial cairn?' I asked.

John drew a small cross in black ink on a 5,000-metre contour above a small settlement called Bibre. 'I'm not entirely sure, but you see this wide space between the contours . . . showing where the land flattens out . . . this is most likely where we built it. It was nearly forty years ago, but I think this is right.'

I was so excited to think that I would be following in Gerry's footsteps.

By late April the weather had improved, and we were ready to head for the mountains again. Paul drove us to Glen Nevis and parked at Polldubh, the end of the road. A confidence-boosting signpost warning 'Danger of Death' indicated the start of the rugged, but popular, path for tourists. It was a shady walk under deciduous woodland, and a busy river rushed through the glen, carving rock into waterfalls and pools. Sunshine warmed our skin as soon as the trail opened out onto the green valley floor and its light glinted and danced as it caught spray from Steall Falls, its water cascading 120 metres down broken cliffs like the swishing tail of a white horse. I could imagine some kind of period drama being filmed here. It felt romantic and old-worldly as we made our way up the broad expanse of the U-shaped valley backed by the Mamores. Crossing a bridge, we investigated some ruins, a sad reminder of when the upper part of the glen was once inhabited; it was another of those places steeped in history and I imagined what life must have been like for the people who lived here. After checking the map we followed a faint but then clear path that ran along the left side of a tributary stream.

'Yeah, if we stick to the river it'll take us right up to the col between Carn Mor Dearg and Aonach Mor,' Paul said.

'Cool, let's go,' I answered, pleased that my boyfriend was enjoying leading for once.

It was warm work climbing higher, but we enjoyed a little respite when we arrived into the glacially scooped-out corrie bowl.
Mountain peaks were holding on to their snows, and meltwaters
were making the ground underfoot wet and sloppy. Repeated footfall
had teased the suggestion of a wandering line through the grasses,
but traces of previous human passage soon disappeared completely.
We followed the meandering river and traipsed over straw-coloured
tufts and heathers on intervening slopes towards views of the broken
terraced cliffs of Carn Mor Dearg. I came across a lost black cap.

'Hey, Paul, look, someone has trodden the exact same way
as us!' I exclaimed, as I waggled it about. 'Life is a bit like route-
finding on a mountain, isn't it? All of us just trying to beat the line
of least resistance,' I said. 'When Mel and I were walking yesterday we met a guy who described these mountains as "dull" and
"a slog" and "not the most interesting of the four thousanders".
I couldn't disagree more. I know the terrain isn't so challenging,
but the views make up for that tenfold, don't you think? They
make me feel so ALIVE!'

'Maybe the guy experienced these hills on a cloudy day,' Paul
suggested, as we trudged on up through a patch of crispy snow
to the col between Carn Mor Dearg and the great wall formed by
the western slopes of Aonach Mor. Steep, grassy crags confronted
us and we stood in silent contemplation.

'It didn't look that bad from down there,' I said.

'No,' Paul agreed, 'and I'm not seeing a path of any sorts. I
think we're just going to have to go straight up.' We scrambled up
the vertiginous wall, clutching at dry, crackly mosses and grasses.
Paul was enjoying himself.

But it was as we were gaily tramping across the snow-covered col towards the second Munro, Aonach Beag, at 1,234 metres, when Paul suddenly said in a very girly octave:

'Eh, Sarah . . . we're walkin' on air.'

'What?'

'There's a golf-ball sized hole here that I can't see the bottom of. Just rocks all the way down at the base of the mountain. I think we need to move over very carefully, we're out on the edge!'

The ground beneath my feet felt solid to me, but I immediately turned and walked through ninety degrees. Once on safer ground, we stopped on an ice-clad outcrop to look back down over the col.

'You can see the sink line, look!' Paul said.

Sure enough, we had been walking on a cornice – literally just an extended lip of snow hanging over the edge of the mountain. Not really what you want to be doing unless dicing with certain death is your thing. If conditions had been milder and the snow just a bit more rotten, our combined weight could have broken through that snowy shelf and we'd have fallen to our doom. It was quite a thought.

'That'll be another of my nine lives blowing five sheets to the wind!' I said.

'I reckon the snow we were walking on was a bit deeper than the length of my body,' Paul mused. I shuddered at the thought.

A low hum of chopper blades broke our silence. The search-and-rescue helicopter was hovering around the vicinity of Ben Nevis, one more reminder of how dangerous the Scottish mountains can be.

We marched back out along the path, which was now busy with tourists of all nationalities: there were girls sweating off layers of make-up and wearing pumps on their feet; a young buck in flip-flops; and a man carrying a new baby in a papoose. I thought about the slippery rocks and water slide they'd had to cross and was glad none of them had come a cropper. 'Maybe they didn't notice the warning sign,' said Paul, as though reading my mind. And then, as we passed back under the deciduous trees, we were stopped by Mountain Rescue. An elderly Indian lady had slipped and knocked herself unconscious against the rocks; her worried and tearful husband sat on the damp ground cradling her head in his lap. It was a disturbing scene after the day's events.

My mind turned to Nepal. Only yesterday, 18 April, news had been broadcast of tragedy in the Himalayas. I had listened in horror to the story as it revealed the highest death toll on one day in the history of mountaineering had taken place. A block of ice – reportedly equalling the weight of 657 buses – broke away from a hanging glacier on Everest's west wall, causing an avalanche to barrel down across the full width of Khumbu Icefall. Sixteen Sherpa died, one of them belonging to the Jagged Globe team. I could hardly believe it. In addition to my tailored plan to locate Nuptse Base Camp, a trek to Everest Base Camp was part of the company's planned itinerary, and I wondered whether we would still go there – or in fact if the trek would go ahead at all. But, after a call from Jagged Globe, I learnt that the trek I had booked was going ahead as planned.

A month would be the longest I'd ever been away from my children and, though they would be well looked after, it didn't stop me feeling guilty about leaving them.

As we said our farewells, Leon put his arms around me.

'Mummy. I'm going to miss you. I'm frightened you won't come back.'

'Aww, what makes you think that, you silly billy?' I said, hugging him tight.

'You told me Gerry died on the mountain and that's where you're going to take Granny's ashes and I don't want you to die too,' he spilt out in one breath, tears rolling down perfectly smooth cheeks.

'Listen. You don't need to worry about me. I'm not going *up* the mountain, just to the bottom of it. I'll be quite safe, I promise. How about I give you a copy of the trek itinerary? That way you will know where I'll be each day.'

Nodding his head, he seemed reassured.

I had felt like a child waiting for Christmas, but finally Paul and I were at the start of our journey to Nepal. We'd left Leon with his grandparents, but Marcus would be staying with one of my neighbours – the same kindly woman who had helped me so much when I'd broken my ankle – and they were both standing on the shingle beach near the airport. As I peered through the aircraft's window I could just make Marcus out, a tiny red dot against the grey, pebbly shoreline. He'd told me he was going to wave till the aeroplane disappeared into the cloud.

See you soon, my lovely boys.

CHAPTER TWENTY

Early Illness

Kathmandu, Lukla and on to Monjo, 2–4 May 2014

I had been especially concerned about carrying the urn with my mother's ashes into Nepal, unsure of whether it was legal or not, and worried my head with ideas that the ashes might be confiscated. So it was with enormous relief and great elation that we made it to Kathmandu via Delhi with all our kit, including the urn, without a hitch. Stepping out into the intense humidity, confusion and noise of a hundred voices competing for taxi fares, Paul spotted a Nepali waving a Jagged Globe sign. He beckoned us over to his waiting taxi. To my amusement, a local asked if he could take a photo of my holdall.

'Yeah, sure!' I said, smiling.

'Thanks, lady.'

'No problem, but then you give me one dollar!' I joked.

The journey between the airport and our hotel was quite exciting. It was a case of every man for himself, and I learnt that road markings really didn't matter. 'They're just guidelines,' our driver said breezily, with a wave of his hand and a toothy grin. People and cows strolled across roads among the moving vehicular mayhem, competing with rows of meandering mopeds and rickshaws in a calamitous cacophony of peeps, toots and honks. The sun's rays filtered through filaments of dust and dirt that hung on thick, warm air, and the overpowering smell of car fumes filled my nostrils. The streets were a colourful, seething mass of humanity. High-rise buildings sandwiched row after row of long narrow corridors in a seemingly endless maze. Black power cables hanging between poles, some slung as low as a skipping rope, were all wrapped in a chaotic mess like giant liquorice wheels on the top of their dodgy wooden supports.

On arrival at the Summit Hotel we were greeted by Mara. 'Our extreme tour guide Barbie,' whispered Paul. I stifled a giggle as she shook my hand and pointed us towards a straw-roofed gazebo outside the reception, where the rest of the trekking team members sat waiting.

'We'll do a little ice-breaker,' she said in a lilting American accent, 'where we'll take it in turns to introduce ourselves and you can share with the rest of the group what your motivations are for coming to Nepal . . .'

'Why's she makin' us tell our reasons for coming out here? She knows perfectly well why each of us has come – it's on our forms. I'm not telling a bunch of strangers about my mum!' I whispered in a hushed tone to Paul.

'I'll go first. So my name is Mara Larson, I'm originally from Oregon. I used to work for NASA studying the effects of altitude on climbers, but now I work for Jagged Globe and am based in Chamonix in France. I've come out here to lead our group on the

Three Peaks, Three Passes trek. There is a lot of information I need to share with the group about our trek which I'll pass on as we go, but one important rule we will be following is: walk high, sleep low. On the trail when we arrive at our stops for the night we'll take a short trip to a higher elevation before returning back down to our camp. This is going to help with the acclimatisation process, but I'll tell you more about all that later.' Mara was in her early thirties, and petite. She was as intelligent as she was attractive and seemed lively and interesting. And so the monologues began . . .

When it came to my turn, red-faced and feeling horribly awkward I garbled my spiel, looking to Paul's face for reassurance. I felt clumsy and embarrassed at my efforts to speak to the group of strangers, 'Your turn, Paul,' I said with haste.

'Hi, I'm Paul and I'm here 'cause of Sarah.' That was it! Short and bloody sweet! He really didn't care what anybody else thought about him. Whispering into my ear, he said, 'Can't be arsed wi' all this Americanised ice-breaker pish.' His was my brand of humour, and being with him gave me extra confidence. I was glad he had come with me.

At dinner we met three guys from Jagged Globe's Everest expedition who had just returned from Base Camp. We sat next to the expedition cook, an Australian. 'The camp has been all but evacuated. There are just porters there now, ferrying equipment and gear down,' he said. 'It was hell being there when the avalanche hit. Everyone was shell-shocked when the number of corpses on the mountain kept rising, and even now, back in civilisation, it's still difficult to come to terms with.'

I understood his bewilderment and grief. After all, I was here to visit the scene of a tragedy that had unfolded almost forty years earlier whose repercussions had vibrated throughout my mother's life and mine.

The hour was getting late, and since we had a five o'clock start Paul and I bade goodnight to our fellow trekkers. 'Make sure you sit on the left side of the plane when you fly out; you'll get a great view of Everest,' the Australian said.

At the airport the next morning, Mara prepared us for a delay due to poor weather, but after only a short wait we got lucky with a weather window. In a rush of frenzied activity we were herded out onto the tarmac towards a tiny Tara airplane. There were only single seats down either side of the aisle, but I got myself a perch on the left-hand side up front, directly behind the pilot. Any misgivings I'd had because of what I'd heard about the flight were quickly dispelled. It wasn't at all scary. Paul pointed out the notice fixed to the entrance of the cockpit which warned, 'Pilots beware, the clouds have rocks in them.' We grinned at each other.

The aircraft took us over the foothills, passing through and in between the cultivated high valley walls. Tiny dwellings far below were merely suggestions as a heat haze softened edges and paled the landscape into a palette of pastel shades; higher up, the clouds drifted apart to reveal fleeting glimpses of Everest. I felt a flurry of anticipation. The flight had been thrilling, but the landing was startling as the small plane hit the runway. The landing strip was only 460 metres long – basically, just long enough to apply the brakes, with no room for pilot error. My eyes were like saucers, my knuckles white and my heart was in my mouth as we approached the brick wall at the end of the short runway at a speed that was faster than felt safe, but the pilot turned the plane assuredly and neatly into the holding area where there was room for just four of these small aircraft.

Disembarking, I was instantly struck by the pure, uncontaminated air here at 2,860 metres. Apart from the aircraft there were no motorised vehicles of any kind here. There weren't even any bicycles. Dirt track of random rubble cobbled together only supported passengers of the two- or four-legged variety. Modest dwellings, with colourful washing spread out to dry on walls, lay cradled in the arms of this high valley. After a short tea break – while our gear was being divvied up between the porters – we set out on our trek in a northerly direction from Lukla. As we passed down a rugged track through a rocky gorge made damp and dark by overhanging branches, the boulder-strewn Dudh Kosi river churned white and milky. It was enchanting.

Oblivious to our presence, young local girls dressed in Western clothes were practising a traditional dance routine while boys on a lower terrace played a variation of cricket. I wondered how many balls they must have lost down the side of the valley to another that lay thousands of feet below. Wonderful, musky scents filled my lungs and a porter passed me by in flip-flops with a staggering load tethered to his back; it included a large box of Nestlé Everyday Milk Powder, a large sack of Crown Rice, four boxes of cans of San Miguel and two larger boxes of bottles of San Miguel. I made a pact with myself that I would not dare to complain about the weight in my backpack. We passed some Buddhist prayer wheels. 'Give them three full spins in the direction of travel to bring good fortune and health,' said Dawa, one of our Sherpa guides. I later wished I'd pushed those wheels with more conviction.

The green landscape was lush and teeming with life. A cacophony of bird calls filled the air; one sounded like a whistle blowing evenly three times, while another shrill call came like a warning, '*Take care!*'

Phakding was at a lower elevation than Lukla and would be our first overnight stop on the trek. We'd only been on the go for a couple of hours and neither Paul nor I could believe our day's walking was over so soon, but we realised the slow pace and early stops were part of the acclimatisation process – annoying but necessary. As we entered the small village it was still raining hard. Two tents stood erected on a terrace below the teahouse in which we now took shelter.

'Fuck,' said Paul dismally, as we stared out from the window down to the orange nylon shelters, 'I don't have to go and put up our tent in that, do I?'

I laughed at him. 'No, ya tool, the porters put the tents up for us!'

With a look of relief, Paul returned his gaze to the rainy scene. 'No wonder they abandoned putting up the rest of the tents.'

It truly was a torrential downpour, but not an early arrival of the monsoons, we hoped. In the end we spent the night in the teahouse. Our accommodation was spartan, but at least we were inside and dry. After we had consumed a thin tomato and garlic soup, *dal bhat* (a traditional Nepalese dish of rice and lentils) and some pineapple, Mara asked us to exchange our high and low points of the day. Then we were introduced to our supporting team: kitchen porters, cook, Sherpa guide and Sirdar, the Sherpa in command of all the staff.

At nine o'clock Paul and I turned in, but I woke in the small hours feeling not quite right. Hoping the sensation of nausea would disappear, I turned over in my sleeping bag and tried to concentrate my worries on any fleas or lice that might be trying to crawl into the bag with me – a nugget of paranoia stemming from a delightfully vivid paragraph in Jon Krakauer's *Into Thin Air*. But itchy bedtime companions were to be the least of my concerns for now.

I woke feeling like death. Creeping from our room as quickly and silently as possible, I made my way down the creaky corridor and locked myself in the toilet, the first non-Westernised loo of the trip so far. I stared down at the dark, rectangular hole in the floor and swiftly planked my feet either side of the pee-stained wood. 'Hello long-drop, old friend,' I muttered as the whole world exploded out of my ass.

Repacking my belongings in preparation for the day's trek to Namche Bazaar was a gargantuan and laboured task as I attempted to keep feelings of nausea under control. As ready as I could be, I took my holdall and backpack downstairs into the dingy light of the dining area. The air was stifling and loaded with smells of cooked breakfast mingling with juniper from an early-morning *puja*, a prayer ritual. I had to get out of there. Sitting on the whitewashed ledge under the window, I held my head in my hands.

'Is everything okay?' Mara asked, as she wandered out from the teahouse.

I had to be honest. 'I'm feeling pretty sick and I've had diarrhoea.'

'Try getting some porridge down, and let's reduce the contents of your daypack so you're carrying less weight,' Mara said. I agreed to her conditions, glad that she wasn't banning me from continuing the journey altogether.

Last to leave the teahouse, I made my way over a short suspension bridge that was gaily adorned with colourful prayer flags, and *khada* – white silk scarves that symbolise the pure heart of the giver and are presented to bring good luck and fortune. The chain bridge bounced and swayed with every step, my stomach churning and my head becoming dizzy. I made it across, but succumbed to the sensation of sickness. Staggering to the edge of the trail, I noticed the steep-sided drop. There was nothing much to grasp on to as I leant forward. My middle and index fingers pressed into the bark of a small, thin tree growing out from the verge as volumes of warm fluid surged up and forced their way out of my mouth like a violent demon being exorcised from my body. Dawa Sherpa made a call and soon Chote, our Sirdar, and Paul appeared. They walked the trail with me. Dawa and Chote seemed concerned, but Paul took my photograph. 'I've never seen anyone actually look like death warmed up,' he said, but I wasn't interested in his attempt to make me smile. Everyone else was waiting higher up. When we rejoined the group they all asked how I was, but I felt so ill I couldn't muster the energy to give even a monosyllabic answer.

Hampered as I was by waves of sickness, my progress up into the valley was slow. I made it to the next small village but, without warning, threw up all over somebody's wall.

'Where's a toilet?' I groaned. Dawa pointed me in the direction of the wall owner's long-drop. 'Paul, come hold the door,' I whimpered desperately as I made my mad dash, 'I won't get it shut in time.'

As I raced towards the wooden structure I caught a glimpse of the Nepalese national bird, the Himalayan monal; it was as fast at disappearing into the bush as the shit was at spraying out my ass. It was a mortifying situation, not least because I'd puked over some poor sod's property, and Paul was now getting to know me really well, subjected as he was to my stinking, noisy bodily expulsions. But at this point I was far too sick to register or care about any embarrassment.

Managing another four miles of trail over 327 metres of ascent, I arrived at Monjo, where Mara took me aside.

'Sarah, the rest of the group have gone on to Namche Bazaar, but you are going no further today.'

'Okay,' I said, too ill to feel sorry for myself.

'Paul said he's staying with you, and I'm leaving Jangbu Sherpa here. He'll keep in radio contact with me. I want you to start taking antibiotics and Diamox. Try and get some crackers down. If you're feeling better in the morning we'll see you at Namche, but you must try to get some food inside for energy. It's a demanding and relentless hike uphill.' It was all very well her saying that, but anything that passed my lips immediately exited from either one end or the other. Things weren't looking good.

Paul was worried about me. He paid for us to stay in a luxury room at the Monjo teahouse. It had a shower – no running hot water – but a shower nonetheless, and a Western toilet. I wondered if it was the toilet that gave it its luxury status or the shower. Either way it didn't matter; I had little time to muse over the triviality since I spent the entire afternoon shitting and puking simultaneously between toilet and sink. *Maybe it's the mirror above the sink that makes it a luxury room.* I lifted my head after the last lot of retching had finished.

'Oh my God! I'm *green*!' I squeaked, as I caught sight of my face for the first time that day.

'I know,' said Paul as he held my hair back with one hand and scooped the plughole clear of my sick with the other.

'I'll clean that!' I said, feeling horrified for the millionth time.

'Don't be daft,' he said gently. 'Go lie down.'

Just then there was a knock at the door and I opened it to see Neil, the youngest member of our group, standing there.

'Paul, look! Neil's green too!' I said without so much as a hello and sounding more cheerful than sympathetic.

'What happened?' Paul asked him.

'I'd continued along the trail with the others but Mara turned me round after I threw up. I'm feeling pretty ropey. I just wanted to let you guys know I'm here. I'm in the room next door. Hopefully it's just a twenty-four-hour thing. Maybe see you later,' Neil replied.

I crossed the room to my bed, lay down inside my sleeping bag and closed my eyes. Though it was a relief to know I was not alone in illness, fear plagued me. If I wasn't fit enough by morning the trek would be over before it had even begun. I couldn't let that happen. I would not let my mum down.

CHAPTER TWENTY-ONE

Onwards and Upwards

To Namche, Thyangboche, Dingboche, 5–7 May 2014

I woke to darkness. Looking across the room I could see that Paul wasn't in his bed. I lay for a while wondering what time it could be. I'd no idea how long I'd been asleep. Crackers sat in their torn packet on the small cabinet next to the bed. Leaning up on my elbow, I reached for them and ate one, then two, a third and then a fourth – this was progress. *Do I feel better? I think I might do!*

Hankering after a Coke, craving the thought of its sugar, I sat on the edge of my bed, slid my feet into their boots without bothering to tie the laces and, rising oh so delicately, made my way to the teahouse dining room. A chill made me shudder as I walked along the narrow wooden corridor. On my right, single-glazed windows offered shadowy views of tall, leafy vegetation on the valley's hillside, which dropped away into complete blackness, and a draught sneaked in through ill-fitting frames. Loud chatter, laughter and gaiety filled the brightly lit dining room on my left. *Where had all those people come from? And where's Paul?*

When I opened the door I was almost knocked straight back out into the night by the overpowering aroma of garlic and spices. *Keep the sickness down. Find Paul. Get Coke. Leave.* Pulling my buff up over my mouth and nose to block out smells, I squeezed my way past rows of occupied seats, my eyes searching faces until I spotted him. I yanked the buff down just long enough to give him a faint smile and ask if he'd get me a Coke. 'I gotta get outta here . . . sorry,' I trailed off. My exit was swift, but I'd clocked Neil sitting next to Paul, baseball cap pulled down hard on his head, properly scoffing his food down. Returning to the room, I felt more than a little envious of his evident recovery and wondered why it was that I was still suffering.

Paul brought me the bottle of Coke. I wanted it there and then, but gave it a good shake before releasing its cap slowly and repeating the process.

'What are you doing?' Paul asked.

'When I went trekking in Peru, I'd been drinking mostly coca tea and water, but on the last day of my travels, at a place near Lake Titicaca, I bought a bottle of Inca Cola. It was neon-yellow and tasted amazing, and I didn't think twice about finishing the bottle quite quickly. It was only when I boarded my flight from Juliaca airport that I began to suffer murderous pains in my stomach – pains so bad that, as I rested my forehead against the seat in front, I thought I might actually pass out. The plane took off and my stomach became harder and more bloated, the pain increased – and then the farting started, non-stop, lengthy, windy eruptions all the way to Lima,' I said, rolling my eyeballs in my head as I recalled the acute embarrassment I'd felt at the time. 'I was so gassy I could have fuelled the plane all by myself. It was a horrible experience, not least for surrounding passengers, and one that I never wish to experience ever, *ever* again.' Paul was laughing, took the bottle from my hand and shook it vigorously, still laughing.

After a full night's sleep the nausea seemed to have passed. I managed a small bowl of porridge for breakfast, then Paul, Neil, Jangbu and I set off for Namche Bazaar – Jangbu carrying my daypack because I was too weak and pathetic. We walked slowly along: up, down, up and down again, on the stony and dung-littered trail that followed the Dudh Kosi river. I needed to dive behind rocks twice on our way. An Australian girl had already gone up a trench in the hillside. I planned to try to wait till she vacated, but succumbed once more to the gastric urge.

'I'm not looking. Not looking. Just passing. Sorry! I just gotta go!' I called as I rushed past the squatting lass.

'No worries!' she yelled sympathetically.

The highest of two long, steel suspension bridges swayed as we crossed it and I paused briefly to look down at the dizzying drop; the river's roar, deadened by distance, was now a mere purr. It was beautiful. And I felt like utter shit. But I knew that if I could get myself to Namche I would be able to push on with the rest of the trek. I had to!

After two and a half hours we arrived at Namche Bazaar, the Sherpa capital, at a lofty 3,440 metres. On first impressions, as I toiled up stone steps avoiding herds of laden donkeys, the town looked far more built up than it had been when the 1975 Nuptse expedition had passed through. White adobe buildings with pink, green and blue rooftops were crammed together; built on stacked terraces, they were linked by winding steps and narrow, cobbled paving. It was a natural amphitheatre – like a Nepalese version of the view from inside the Colosseum. Yak-dung smoke filled the air. I felt queasy but kept quiet. We passed chattering locals standing in shop doorways. Somewhere nearby a school bell rang and we heard joyous shouts and cries of children as they rushed out to play. The campsite we were using was on a high terrace on the back wall of this scooped-out bowl. We dumped our backpacks into tents that were already set up. Clouds swirled and funnelled upwards from the valley far below as I sat outside enjoying the afternoon warmth. It was good to rest.

Paul had disappeared but came back minutes later with a tube of Pringles. 'Thought you could try these. You need to get something inside,' he said as he handed them over. I took them from him with thanks, not because I wanted to eat them, but because his thoughtfulness made me feel cared for.

Neil, Paul and I had been sitting for a while before the others appeared. 'You guys! You've made it! You have no idea how happy I am to see you all. I really missed you!' said Matt, a film producer from London who had signed up for the trek on a last-minute whim. We'd hit it off from the start.

'What do you reckon, do you think his tolerance of his tent mate may already be wearing thin?' Paul commented. We laughed.

After I managed to eat just a little of my lunch, Paul, Neil and I were taken on a short twenty-minute acclimatisation walk with Jangbu Sherpa above Namche. This was when the high-altitude flatus expulsion reared up. I hung back, letting Neil and Jangbu walk ahead, my eyeballs practically popping their sockets as I felt gas rapidly increase in my stomach. 'I shouldn't have had the Coke,' I groaned to Paul as wind exploded out of my butt. Neil and Jangbu turned round, disbelief on their faces, while mine was full of apology.

Neil and Jangbu bailed, leaving Paul and me alone. There then followed a constant stream of wind as we made our way all around the narrow streets that wound around Namche. I was helpless. It was the horrendous flight from Juliaca to Lima all over again, but my audible suffering did at least cheer some people up as I was given the thumbs up from one American woman passing by.

The clattering of hooves alerted us to the presence of donkeys, and interesting trekkers of all nationalities, in their puffy down jackets and colourful woollen hats, chattered gaily in small groups. It was fascinating to meander along the narrow, cobbled paths. Tables set up either side of darkened shop doorways all sold similar wares: Tibetan prayer wheels, Buddha statuettes, prayer flags, masks, knives, knitted headbands, pretty bead friendship bracelets, rings and necklaces.

Mostly concerned with replenishing my already dwindling supply of baby wipes, we found a small pharmacy, and then stocked up on powdered juice and plain Pringles. It didn't matter that prices in Namche were three times higher than anywhere else in Nepal. After witnessing the enormous loads local porters had to bear to bring the goods there in the first place I wouldn't have grudged having to pay five times the amount. Suddenly, warning cramps creased across my lower abdomen.

'I gotta get to a toilet.'

'Let's go in there then.'

Paul pointed to a café and we trotted up the stairs. We stayed there for a while. Two documentaries were being screened. The first was about the real heroes of Everest, the Sherpa. The second film, incredibly, was about the avalanche that had killed the sixteen climbing Sherpa during April. I was surprised it was being aired just weeks after the tragedy. The Discovery Channel's crew were at Base Camp to film the American Joby Ogwyn, whose plan it was to jump from Everest's summit in a wing suit and land at Base Camp. Filming had started two weeks before the avalanche and had documented the *puja* ceremonies and the camaraderie between Sherpa and Westerner, then footage of the disaster was caught on film.

Helicopters flew in to what they call the football pitch – a flat area of snow the size of a putting green – and were operating at their very limits for the rescue operation. Although they can fly at greater altitudes, they are unable to hover because the air is too thin. Corpses were dug out and airlifted off the mountain, but three still remained undiscovered. The last body to be recovered by rescuers was recorded on film. I couldn't believe what I was seeing. The lifeless leg and foot of Dorje Sherpa stuck up out of the snow and the team dug out his body. It was harrowing, but my eyes remained transfixed to the screen. When it finished Paul and I sat in a stunned silence for a moment. 'I wonder how the families of the dead Sherpa will survive?' I said, trying not to cry.

I was ill, and now my spirits were even lower. I felt weighed down by the sadness of everything. I thought about the avalanche victims and their families, I thought about all the people who must have died and been left on the mountains, I thought about Gerry, and I thought about my mum.

The sickness had stopped, but none of my dinner was digested; instead it passed straight through me. After sharing high and low points of the day with the rest of the group, Paul and I went off to bed. I read some of *Greenvoe* by George Mackay Brown, the only book I had brought with me on the trek. My eyes didn't stay open for long, but sleep didn't last. Like gumballs being released from a vending machine, one fart was followed immediately by the rattle and rumble of the next; it was relentless. After an already upsetting day I started to feel even more down and pondered whether there might be such a thing as death by farts. I looked across at Paul, he hadn't stirred. With only my thoughts and the long-drop toilet for company it was a long and dreadful night.

Kongde's crisp, snowy outline against the blue sky was dazzling as I unzipped the tent. I admired its vast scale, but it didn't take long before clouds started to conceal the view, yet again making the mountain seem theatrical and full of visual trickery.

At breakfast Mara gave us a briefing. 'I've received an updated report. The weather conditions aren't conducive to our original planned itinerary, so I've decided to reverse our route. Instead of trekking to Gokyo we will head for Chukhung. If anyone else suffers early illness there are more opportunities for recovery with an option to regroup further along on the trail.'

That seemed a logical plan, but I also felt a private sense of elation because going to Chukhung first meant that I might be able to deliver my mum to Gerry on the exact anniversary of his death. I'd chosen to do the trek in May because it was the same time Gerry had been here and I'd understood our route would take us past the Nuptse valley, where his body still lay entombed in its icy grave, a couple of weeks after 9 May – the day he had died. But now the change of itinerary meant that I might reach the valley on the anniversary itself, which would make the scattering of Mum's ashes even more meaningful and perfect.

En route to Deboche at 3,820 metres, we travelled in a north-easterly direction, a gently ascending traverse. Sitting at the side of the trail on a white plastic chair was a Tibetan lama, a Buddhist monk. An open box sat on top of a table into which a 'non-obligatory' obligatory donation was made by each of us – for this, we received his holiness's blessing for our onward journey. I willingly paid my dues, figuring I needed all the help I could get.

A short distance further along the dusty trail, and fenced off, was a large, white Buddhist shrine, known as a chorten monument, crowned with a golden top and shaped like a giant Tibetan meditation bell. It was built for all Sherpa and in honour of the Nepali mountaineer Tenzing Norgay. A Himalayan griffon soared on the thermals in the sky above.

Birdsong filled the air as we descended through birch draped in old man's beard. Rhododendron forests were in bloom with delicate pink and white flowers.

I waggled my camera at a local lad, who let me take his photograph.

'I can't wait to show this picture to Marcus and Leon,' I said to Paul. 'How old are you?' I asked the boy.

'Fourteen,' he replied, before strapping three pieces of ply-wood onto his back that were more than one and a half times his height, and the width of a large doorway. The boy set off, always remaining ahead of us along the trail. It was impressive but also humbling to witness.

As we passed through more rhododendron forest I soon saw that these load-bearing skills were developed from a young age. A sturdy-legged eight-year-old in a worn black down jacket torn at the armpit, muddied cotton trousers and a pair of rubber open-toed sandals scuttled past. He was bent almost double under the weight of a large sack, which was attached to his back by a cloth sling fixed around his forehead. Dawa told me the boy was preparing for a future as a porter, with aspirations to become a Sherpa and one day a Sirdar. *Meanwhile a few thousand miles away Marcus and Leon are probably bending their forefingers and thumbs out of shape on their Xbox consoles.* These Nepalese youngsters were living a hard but honest life and I couldn't help but feel inspired, even though their futures probably held the dangers of work at high altitude.

We stopped for lunch. It was noodle soup and beans. 'If you eat the beans, stay away from me,' Paul said, with a look of such consternation it made me laugh. He needn't have worried. I couldn't eat anything other than the Pringles.

From our lunch spot it was an hour-and-three-quarter slow-paced walk, under the cover of low cloud, up to Thyangboche at 3,860 metres. We crossed another high and lengthy suspension bridge, which sagged in the middle as it supported the weight of a yak caravan carrying expedition holdalls, barrels and other gear. A sliver of silver far below, the Dudh Kosi frothed, its rapid flow hushed by steep valley walls supporting stands of aromatic pines. As we continued high on the trail in single file Paul, who had been walking in front of me, suddenly turned round and virtually winded me with a punch in the stomach.

'Check that out!' he said excitedly, 'it's like a giant barn owl. You see it? On the rock ahead. Look!'

'Wow! What is that?' Closer inspection revealed it was only the kitchen porter's load resting against a rock. *Muppet.*

As the trail climbed high and dropped low, many chortens dotted each side of the trail and a never-ending stream of laden yak made their journey alongside the river. Thyangboche, one of the most famous monasteries in all Nepal, was shrouded in cloud when we arrived. It felt mystical. Digging out the diary from its place in my rucksack, I looked at a photo of this spot from 1975. Before I'd left Scotland, John Peacock had emailed photographs of the expedition's journey to me and I'd printed them out. My plan was to take photographs from the same places so that on return I could show John how things had changed – or perhaps how they had stayed the same. In comparison with the photograph, the monastery was unrecognisable. I had to double-check we were actually at the same place, so I asked Dawa. 'Yes, this is Thyangboche,' he answered.

Prayer wheels were built onto the top of a wall flanking each side of an ornate gateway. Beyond the courtyard, at the top of several narrowing flights of steps, the temple sat squarely. Heavy brown curtains, hung down over the pink brick walls, parted to reveal the way inside. We took off our boots and entered the garishly coloured place of worship with its many carvings and massive central statue of Buddha. We watched as a lone Tibetan monk in burgundy robes finished chanting, rose from his cross-legged position and left: I felt like I'd intruded. I was fascinated by how dramatically different the monastery was and wanted to find out about the changes. Stepping back outside, I felt the cold. Paul and I went to the nearby bakery, where a warm drink didn't help to heat us up much, but our Sirdar, Chote, was sitting at one of the tables. I showed him my photographs.

'What happened to the monastery?' I asked.

'When was this taken?' Chote queried, studying the images.

'1975.'

'Ah, well. The monastery was reduced to rubble during an earthquake in 1933 and was rebuilt. Then in 1989 it was destroyed again by fire. All historical and spiritual treasures were lost, but the Sherpa people came together, like they did before, and gave their labour and craftsmanship to rebuild it,' said Chote. I was yet again impressed by the people, their faith and resilience. In the face of loss and adversity they did not give up. Their determination was something I felt I understood.

As we left Thyangboche the clouds broke up long enough to afford a fleeting view of Lhotse but, like unwrapped gifts, Nuptse and Everest remained hidden from sight for now. Our lower campsite for the night was at Deboche, half an hour's walk from the monastery. Feeling super-tired after dinner, Paul and I called it a night. Although it was only half past seven it was already dark as we snuggled into our sleeping bags.

'Hey, Paul,' I whispered.

'Hey, Sarah,' he whispered back.

'Night night, sleep tight, mind the bed bugs don't bite!'

Talk about famous last words. I woke the next morning with rapidly swelling and ragingly itchy welts that were spreading over my body right before my eyes. Unbelievable! Every scrap of food that passed my lips was still exiting faster than a Fedex delivery; I had suffered smelly and incessant attacks of knicker-staining flatulence; and now it seemed I was being ravaged by fleas. After I'd already gone to the effort of packing up my sleeping bag and mat, both now had to be unrolled, beaten and aired. My infested clothing was bagged up and, using bowls of water, I had to wash my entire self from head to toe – it did feel bloody brilliant to have clean hair and put on fresh clothes though. *I should have spun those prayer wheels harder.*

The altitude began to have its effects. Paul had woken through the night feeling as if the back of his head had been whacked by a cricket bat. My headaches came and went, and we both felt mildly sick and floaty. The trail was not technically difficult as we followed its age-old route, but the thinning air slowed our group and silenced all. In single file we made tracks above the Imja Khola river, where a large metal bridge lay collapsed and broken. Paul disappeared behind it.

'Paul, what are you doing?' Mara asked.

'Errrr . . . I really gotta go,' Paul tried to explain.

'Can you try to hold on? This place isn't safe, there's objective danger of rockfall here. It's best to keep moving.'

Paul obediently complied, but as we continued on the steep, narrow trail contouring high on the valley hillside, and because he was ahead of me, I noticed he was walking funny.

'Are you okay?' I asked.

'Nope. I think I've shat myself and I can't check 'cause there's no fucking rocks or bushes to go behind.' I felt so sorry for him – but also slightly relieved that at least I didn't have to feel so embarrassed about my own display of bodily functions.

There was not much in the way of distraction from our symptoms; billowing white clouds obscured any morning views of big mountains, and valley hillsides began to shed their colour as we climbed higher up out of the treeline into a monochromatic landscape of greys and browns. The Imja Khola zigzagged along the V-shaped valley floor and, like the paths of lava flow from a volcanic eruption, massive rockfalls scarred the opposite hillside – a lasting memory of previous monsoons. A man was negotiating his way along the lower scree slopes on the opposite hillside, while another drove a herd of yak across a higher path. Watching them travel temporarily took my mind off how grotty I was beginning to feel.

After passing yet another chorten and admiring a long line of tilted *mani* prayer stones, I thought it would be a good time to talk to our trek leader.

'Hey, Mara, I know you'll have been told that I have asked for the trek to be tailored for me and I was just wondering how that's going to work.'

'Yeah, I read in your application that you wanted to go find Nuptse Base Camp. Was it your father that was a climber?'

I explained my relation to Gerry, about his summit bid and how he was meant to marry my mum but the accident had claimed his life six weeks before their wedding day.

'Don't worry, I'll speak with Chote Sirdar and we'll get your trek arranged. You know, my boyfriend died on Annapurna's south face. I can totally relate to your sense of needing to go to the place where Gerry's body lies.'

She talked at length, and I was touched that she had told me about her boyfriend so I decided to tell her my whole story: that I had brought my mother's ashes with me.

'That's amazing. You should write a book!' she said.

'Maybe I will,' I laughed.

Dingboche village was still a further two hours away. The thinning air was cold, dry and causing shortening of breath. The going was hard. We all wore neckerchiefs over our noses and mouths to protect our skin from the ultraviolet rays, and also to help prevent the dusty, dry air from giving us the renowned Khumbu cough. It was a relief finally to see a modest collection of teahouses come into view; we would have an extra day and night's acclimatisation here – and I for one was grateful for the rest. That evening dinner was pizza, chips and spaghetti with a tomato sauce followed by delicious apple, and for the first time in ages I was actually able to enjoy what I had been given. The antibiotics at last seemed to be working.

As I lay in my sleeping bag I said a silent and wholly selfish prayer: *Dear God, Please let me get a great sleep. I've been running on empty and haven't had a non-trekking day since I've been ill. I really need to be fit and well so I can take my mum to Gerry. Amen.*

God must have been listening. I woke up the following morning feeling awesome. Even the skies were a cheerful blue.

I took photos of the mountains; like wintry queens, they were resplendent in their glittering white cloaks. Icy fluting thrust upwards like giant folds while plumes of spindrift from the highest peaks blew from summit crests like delicate trains. Clouds were being born: the sun their sire, and the mountains their dame!

At breakfast I ate all my porridge and had a pancake with lots of apple jam then chilled out on a chair in the dusty courtyard to take in the view. Straight ahead, soaring to 6,812 metres, was Ama Dablam – possibly the most perfect mountain I'd ever seen. Its lower reaches were blocked from sight by the green, corrugated long-drop toilet that was built on top of eight stone steps, and in front it, piled up high, was a giant, dome-shaped mound of yak dung drying in the sun.

'It's an incredible mountain, isn't it?' said Paul as he came and sat on the chair next to me.

'Yeah,' I replied, nodding towards the toilet and dung with a smile, 'But there's always gotta be some kinda shit to spoil things . . . yak shit . . . get it?'

'You're obviously on the mend,' he said with a broad grin.

My hand in his, we took a leisurely walk up the main street of Dingboche, a precarious, pot-holed thread of dirt. A narrow channel of none-too-clean-looking water ran its length. It was piped up from the river below, and locals were using a bucket to scoop out water to use for cooking, washing and drinking. Busy at work behind a low dry-stone dyke wall, a large woman in a long pink skirt, apron, blue top and headscarf was flinging yak muck across her land, and as we ventured further more mountains revealed themselves. Island Peak with its brown triangular face looked dwarfed by its neighbour, Lhotse.

'Gerry climbed Island Peak in one day. Maybe we could come back here to climb it too?'

'Anything's possible,' said Paul.

I felt excited. I wanted to go everywhere Gerry had been, to see the landscape as he might have seen it. As I had felt in the Scottish hills, and on the rock in North Wales, it somehow made me feel closer to him and therefore my mum.

Returning through the village, we found an open kiosk. It was the largest store there and only the size of a two-door wardrobe, but among its variety of useful items, and with Mum and Gerry in mind, I purchased a set of prayer flags.

At eleven o'clock Paul, Harry, Dawa and I hiked over the hill to Pheriche while the rest of the group went higher up into the hillside to aid acclimatisation. We were planning to attend the Himalayan Rescue Association (HRA) talk on mountain sickness and how to recognise signs of pulmonary and cerebral oedema. A chorten-splattered hilltop separated the two settlements of Dingboche and Pheriche, and as we approached Pheriche, Dawa spotted a lammergeier, its wide wings stroking the air in an effortless glide. Feeling emotional to have my first sighting of Gerry's favourite bird, I took its sighting as a good sign. Having threaded our way down steep scree to the wide valley floor, we continued along winding dirt paths to the Himalayan Lodge, where we had lunch. Soon after eating Paul was out of sorts.

'That went straight through me. My guts are rank,' he groaned.

'Start on the antibiotics. Here, take mine just now,' I told him firmly.

To kill some time before the talk we wandered around the settlement.

'Have you noticed a pattern with the clouds, Paul?' I asked, as they rose up from the lower valleys, bringing with them strong winds. 'Mornings are often quite clear, but by early afternoon they gather and stampede upwards enveloping everything with their mists.'

He mumbled agreement, but I could tell that he was too distracted by his stomach. And I now became preoccupied with what the clouds were doing. If I stood any chance of finding the memorial cairn my good-weather window would only last till early afternoon. I worried away to myself.

Early evening, back in the teahouse at Dingboche, the porters, Sherpa and Sirdar crowded around a table with John Peacock's map opened out. They pointed at the inked-in cross – where John thought we would locate the memorial cairn. Although I had no comprehension of Nepalese it was clear that Chote was explaining about Gerry and the accident on Nuptse. Many pairs of sympathetic brown eyes looked up at me, but there was something else that I recognised in their gaze, which I tried to ignore – I could tell they didn't think that we were going to find what I was looking for.

CHAPTER TWENTY-TWO

Deliverance

Chukhung, 9–10 May 2014

'Today is the day he died you know,' I said to Paul.

'I know,' he said affectionately, rubbing his thumb against the back of my hand.

We carried on in an easterly direction to Chukhung, at 4,730 metres. Low-growing shrubs were ever sparser and the trail became rockier. And, just when I thought I'd seen the most spectacular perspective of Ama Dablam, I was treated to yet another as we contoured its opposite hillside. Immense hanging glaciers and tiered fluting, luxurious folds and furls, coated the mountain like thick Christmas-cake icing. Ahead were Island Peak, Lhotse and Nuptse, its deadly snow couloir coming increasingly into focus. A continuous series of ridges punctured the skyline like ferociously sharp angular fangs, while luminous peaks stood out against the piercing blue. Studying the mountain faces through binoculars, I marvelled at the vivid creations in ice, sculpted by the elements. It was like looking through a kaleidoscope: a vision of dark, fractured geometrical lines, wedges and coils. Vapour lifted off into the air, twisting and furling like flames, changing the mood and appearance of the landscape. The scene was mesmerising; its wildness resonated within me. *Did Gerry feel this same wonderment? Do you feel it, Mum? I think that you do. And tomorrow, Gerry, we're coming to find you. We are on our way!*

We arrived at Chukhung in time for lunch. Porters had already set up tents in the earthen makeshift camping ground. Our team grouped inside a spectacularly filthy wooden shack whose tables and surfaces were covered in thick layers of dust and cobwebs. It was like a scene in an abandoned railroad house from an old western movie. Soup was served. Rushing our food, Paul and I escaped the dirt and the drone of bluebottles as they bounced off the windowpanes. Out in the fresh air, we descended the stone steps and sat on the dusty wall to wait for the others.

Following the rule of walk high, sleep low, for the first time our whole group left together for a short but steep acclimatisation hike towards the mountain Chukhung Ri. It felt warm in the sunshine when we eventually stopped, and Paul and I sat on a rock as if it were a seat with the gods, taking in the views of our grandiose surroundings. In front of us a castellated horseshoe of serrated peaks like the teeth of a saw glistened brilliantly white against a perfectly blue sky. The grey, blistered tongue of the Ama Dablam Glacier stretched its way to vanishing point down the Chukhung valley. The smell of heathers reminded me of home. Birds sang in the stillness, and butterflies danced frivolously.

'How are you feeling?' asked Paul. 'I'm a bit breathless.'

'I'm okay. I did have a small nagging headache but it seems to be going.'

We didn't speak much. There was no need. We watched as everyone trekked back down the hillside. There was no hurry to leave so we stayed on our rock together, in contemplation of the day, before we too returned to camp. Inside our tent we addressed the ritual unpacking of our holdalls, pumped up our mats and unrolled sleeping bags. I combed through my long, knotted hair while Paul, leaning up on his elbow, watched the battle with a smile. We remained in silence.

Fishing in my bag, I pulled out the set of prayer flags that I'd bought at Dingboche and linked them up, wishing that I was trekking my way to Gerry with them right then. I tried to console myself, as well as prepare for disappointment. *What's one more day in the scheme of things? Even if we don't locate the cairn tomorrow, it doesn't matter. What's important is that I can make my own cairn, drape my flags, say words, and then I can send Mum to find him.* I looked forward to delivering my eulogy – not least because fragments of it were on a perpetual loop in my mind, driving me to distraction.

Chote walked over to wish me well, but his tidings came with a warning. 'I have passed by this place many times and have never seen what you are looking for.'

My heart sank to my stomach. As Chote left I turned to Paul and rested my head against his shoulder.

'Do you think we'll find the cairn?'

'We'll try,' Paul said. I didn't want to think about the possibility of failure. I had to believe that we would find it. Shuffling closer to him in my sleeping bag, I closed my eyes, but my unfulfilled business called out to me like a siren as I drifted towards sleep.

'Wahsheeng waterrrrr!' yelled the kitchen porter outside our tent as 10 May dawned. His voice was alarming, like a giant gong resonating. It was amazing how we made the small basin of tepid water meet our needs. 'Teea!' Dawa called five minutes later, thrusting a hand through the nylon flap and holding out a cup for Paul. 'No tea, *didi*?' he asked – every day, always addressing me using the same term of endearment, meaning 'sister'.

'No, thanks,' I'd reply – every day. Breakfast was at six-thirty, and Chote had decided that Dawa, who spoke better English than Jangbu, was the best candidate to take Paul and me on our mission.

Paul, Dawa and I left, kicking up orange dust with each step. I watched Paul's head bobbing up and down ahead of me. I was glad he was here with me. Our pace was reasonably quick as we ascended the sandy trail, and clouds began to disperse as the day heated up. Contouring the hillside, we followed Dawa mostly in silence; it was taxing enough to draw breath.

'Is Bibre below?' I panted.

'No, it's over the next ridge.'

Although I thought I'd studied the lie of the land well as we'd passed by the day before, I recognised very little: lumps, bumps and scars on the grey landscape – they all looked the same and I realised how reliant we were on Dawa to guide us in the right direction.

'Do you know where we are going?' I asked.

'I've never been up this valley before,' he said, shaking his head. I literally couldn't fucking believe it. When we stopped for a drink, I gave him my map as well as John Peacock's small colour photographs.

'Let's climb up to the top of that ridge; maybe it'll give us a better viewpoint,' I suggested.

We carried on along a faint path which then descended to a dried riverbed of black stones. Waves of optimism came and went. I recalled meeting John the previous summer, when he had spread his old map of the Khumbu Himal across the table in the supermarket café. It had all looked so straightforward then. But here I was, not a large fingertip on a thin contour line, but a small person enclosed in an enormous, ribbed and alien landscape. The only reference point was the mountain itself, Nuptse, towering ahead on our right. Dawa still had the map. My only clue as to where we were, roughly, was when Paul raised his hand, palm out-turned to invite mine.

'High five!' he said.

'Do you know where we are?' I asked excitedly.

'No.'

'Why'd you high-five me then?'

'Because we've reached the 5,000 metres mark,' he answered, tapping the altimeter on his watch. 'That's where the cross was drawn onto the map, isn't it?' We checked the map against the landscape, and sure enough the geographical features looked about right, but the photographs didn't marry up. We discussed where we thought we might be. 'I think we should aim for the "V" shape on the horizon line at the head of the valley,' said Paul. I felt agitated.

'But according to John's cross on the map the cairn should be somewhere around here. I want to go up higher, onto that ridge on the right; maybe we'll see more?' We were penned in on our left by the jagged black rock of Dingogma; its dark, brittle shards, arranged in stacks and chimneys, were a stark contrast to the white of Nuptse, which soared skywards on our right. And the return view of Ama Dablam was imposing and authoritative. I felt tiny in this gigantic arena, and Chote's words haunted me. '*I have passed by this place many times and have never seen what you are looking for.*'

Fitter and better adapted to higher altitude, Dawa raced ahead. Paul and I followed behind across the stony, egg-box terrain. But when I next looked up, Paul was pulling further away from me and Dawa had completely disappeared. Despite my best effort to get his attention Paul was too far ahead, and my voice too small to be heard. Irrationally, I felt vulnerable. Try as I might, I physically couldn't get myself up the damn moraine any faster. Each intake of breath seemed piercing in the rarefied air, my lungs felt like they were going to collapse as they laboured. 'Fucking-fuckity-fuck,' I muttered. 'This is so not cool. Not cool, at all.' I felt panic that I'd be left behind, but had to stop to let my heart regain rhythm so that I could try to get control over my breath in order to yell out. Paul stopped and looked around. *Thank God.*

'Where's Dawa, did you see where he went?' I called. But Paul shook his head. I shouted. 'DAWA!' No answer. I knew he wouldn't have abandoned us and we weren't really lost, but we were in vast surroundings – and I had an important job to do. Minutes seemed like hours.

'He's here!' Paul called. He had topped out and spied Dawa, sitting on a rock poring over the map. Relieved, I puffed up onto the ridge and was suddenly struck by the sight of Nuptse's south face, now in full view. For a moment my unquiet mind became still.

'I think this is the area of the Base Camp,' Dawa said, bringing me back to the present.

I felt elated. 'Will we find the memorial?'

'No,' he said, his soft, brown eyes looking directly into mine, 'I don't think so.' The waves of optimism and deflation tormented me. Turning my head to hide my disappointment, I fixed my gaze along the ridge of lateral moraine. We'd been walking for hours. I gulped at the cold air. Early-afternoon clouds now sat across the base of Ama Dablam; it wouldn't be long before they would conceal our views completely. Time was running out, but I wasn't prepared to give up.

Taking John's photographs, Paul wandered off and so did Dawa. And I just stood and stared at the mountain that changed the course of my mother's, and my, entire life. As I studied the route to its peak I now saw how it was possible that Gerry had fallen all 1,800 metres from its top to the bottom. I glanced around. Paul and Dawa were far enough away. '*Please*, Gerry! Show us the way!' I implored. 'I've brought my mum to you! She's here now.' I knew my pleas could not be answered, but it didn't stop my own superstitious hope. And if his spirit was awakened, I hoped that it leapt with joy.

As I followed Paul, I focused on Nuptse. I could see the bergschrund at its base and wondered if Gerry's body might still be there, perfectly entombed in ice. I wanted to go and find him, but that wish was futile too. The sweeping hands of my watch ticked on, and I resigned myself to the fact that we were not going to locate the memorial cairn. I decided then that where I stood would be as good a place as any to build my own shrine.

I was emotional. How could something so breathtakingly beautiful have been the cause of such untold misery?

'Come here a minute,' Paul called. I turned in his direction. He beckoned me to him. His simple gesture caused another tidal wave of optimism. I tried to suppress the sensation, afraid of disappointment, as I made my way over. Resting his hand upon my shoulder, he pointed down towards an amorphous lump. 'Look down there, can you see it?' I strained my neck forward and screwed up my eyes to scan the scene. Others would scarcely have noticed the collection of rocks piled together against a larger boulder; anyone could be forgiven for missing it, camouflaged as it was. Tears filled my eyes.

'What a wonderful miracle!' I said, the words choking out of my mouth. Against the odds, and down to Paul's perseverance in trying to match up the old photos against the landscape, he had found the memorial cairn.

Already halfway down, Dawa called, 'Be careful, *didi*. It's very steep and loose rocks.'

Swallowing back tears and composing myself, I picked a way down the scree from our high point. I staggered over to a large rock and sat down in a joyous daze. Paul handed over the tiny, crumpled pictures as he joined me: the memorial cairn with Nuptse towering behind, Base Camp with Pokalde in the distance, the Alouette rescue helicopter near Base Camp with Ama Dablam in sharp focus to the south – they all matched up. Base Camp's position was perfectly sensible: right next to a glacial lake, lying at a low point between the big mountains, providing good shelter and situated well enough for the team to view progress on Nuptse through binoculars. Checking the map, I realised how earlier confusion over the memorial cairn's location had arisen – we were just over 3 kilometres north-north-east, and 188 metres higher in elevation, than the little black cross marked on the map. The cairn had stood almost unchanged for thirty-nine years; all that was missing was the aluminium cross.

Following tradition, I placed a rock on top of the cairn, as did Paul. Then, extricating the prayer flags from my bag, I attached one end securely to the base of the cairn while Dawa tied the other to a large boulder at a higher point. Paul and Dawa said nothing at all, respectfully stepped back and went down to the lake. I took the urn from my backpack and carried it to the cairn, Nuptse behind it like a towering tombstone.

Carefully, thoughtfully, I scattered Mum's ashes. I paused briefly, aware and upset that these were the fragmented remains of my mother. 'It's been a long time coming, but I did get there in the end, like you said I would. I can let you go now, and we can both finally be at peace.'

When the cross had been removed, rocks had been displaced and a recess in the centre of the cairn left gaping open – almost as though it was known that I was coming. I placed the urn inside then walked to Paul. He had a photo that I wanted to put into it along with a simple message. Standing back, I could never have imagined a spot in which such perfection, beauty and peace existed. It was an incredible final resting place and I felt confident that it would remain this way, undisturbed for at least another thirty-nine years and more. No words passed our lips. I was touched by the feeling expressed in Dawa's eyes, which he lowered as he walked purposefully by. He set about rebuilding fallen rocks from the cairn with great fervour, blocking in the urn, keeping its secrets preserved for ever. He wasn't Dawa Sherpa any more; he was Dawa my friend, and I was glad I hadn't done all this on my own.

Absorbing the setting, we three sat on a rock and ate some jelly babies, lost in our own thoughts. After all my troubles and failed relationships, feeling as if I'd been wandering aimlessly through life, I was finally confident I was on the right track. I now understood that, like being on a mountain at high altitude, life was a test of endurance. You just had to be patient, and know that no matter how tough things may seem there is always a way through the difficulties. You had to learn to accept the things you couldn't control but be brave enough to change the things you could. My mum's death had hit me hard; I had felt so adrift and alone. But while I would never stop missing her, I could find a way to live with my loss. Giving myself physical challenges had started me on the path to healing. Understanding her life and accepting her death had helped me to understand myself better. And, above all, I came to realise the importance of having people in my life to support me. Now I have a partner who loves me unconditionally, and I have a great friend in Mel. And, of course, I have my children. As I sat there on the rock I wished that I could see them and hug them tightly.

With the weather beginning to close in we had to leave. I thought about John, and how pleased he would be to know that we'd made it. I took a photograph of the empty expedition Base

Camp and lingered, wanting to stay, but having to go. Dawa, Paul and I collected some rocks, small, token reminders of this special place. As we travelled back over the hillside above Chukhung a massive bird of prey glided down the valley. Its colouring and long, wedge-shaped tail were unmistakable. It was the lammergeier, the very bird Gerry had said he would want to be reincarnated as, and I wondered. I thought about the embroidery Mum had stitched for Gerry, her wedding gift, in shiny threads of pink and blue *Today is the First Day of the Rest of Your Life* – and so it was.

Homeward Bound

Ben Nevis — The Venomous Mountain, July 2015

Early June 2014 was warm. Paul and I were back from our trek in Nepal and I was keen to spend as much time as possible with my sons after so long away from them. Hauling out our bikes, we took advantage of the weather and set off to Ardersier.

My legs were on autopilot as we pedalled along. I thought about how I had long wanted to move back to the village where I grew up, to the place where my family had been together, alive and well, when everything had been all right. I thought about how I had talked myself out of the notion, telling myself that going back wouldn't bring them back, and it wouldn't be the same; reminding myself that the clock cannot be turned back. As the wheels on my bike turned I supposed it was enough to at least be within cycling distance of my old home.

Ditching our bikes, the three of us raced up the sandy path, brushing through spiky gorse, to arrive at the viewpoint on top of Cromal Mount. A gentle breeze ruffled through my hair as I stood with hands on hips catching my breath. I swept my gaze across the familiar landscape until my eyes rested their sights upon Inchrye. This time there was none of the sorrow or self-pity that I used to feel when I took in the view of the old family home. I no longer felt embittered by those events of my life that had cast their dark shadows in me. The trapped, lost and lonely girl was gone; I now knew myself. I was my own woman.

Just ten yards further along the road from my childhood home lay a row of seven south-facing terraced houses, their gable ends towards the sea, and in one of the gardens I saw a prominent 'For Sale' sign. When we climbed back down to the bottom of the hill my belly fluttered with a flurry of excitement and I went to take a closer look.

Within a few days I'd made an appointment and returned to view the house. It wasn't big enough for me and two boys. But the owner told me the property next door was twice its size, the owner had recently died, and the daughter was selling.

'Was it Mrs Johnstone who lived there?' I'd asked.

'Yes, that's right. Did you know her?'

'Yeah. I used to live at Inchrye. Her husband Scotty and my grandad were great friends.'

Whether or not the stars were in alignment, the timing was never more right. The final piece of my jigsaw was about to slot into place.

Mrs Johnstone's daughter remembered my family and we talked about the old days as she showed me around the house. 'It's not on the market yet. We're still trying to sort everything out,' she said.

The place was in desperate need of renovation and modernisation, but that didn't matter – it would be a real blank canvas. I could do it up in my own time; there was even room for an art studio where I'd be able to work on the paintings I had started after my accident. The good feeling I had about the house was inspiring, and something told me it was going to be mine.

Within two weeks of putting my own property up for sale a young couple came to view it and soon put in an offer. I was ecstatic, and, with my mortgage secured, the wheels were set in motion.

The last night in our flat was not without its usual disruption. Loud banging and shouts woke us at three in the morning. Looking out into the hallway, I saw and heard nothing. I went to the kitchen and opened the window. There was nobody out on the street far below. As I pulled my head back in I looked up and saw, to my horror, a pair of feet dangling above the window. Voices shouted again.

'C'mon! Don't be daft,' said one.

'You're gonna kill yourself, come back up! We'll help ya,' said another.

'The police'll be here any minute! Get back in, ya fuckin' idiot!' urged another faceless voice.

Leaks, slugs and bad neighbours: for so long it had felt as though we were being driven from the home where I'd wanted to belong with my memories of Mum. But as I closed the door on the flat for the last time I felt no regret. I was so much stronger now: the mountains had made me that way. By this point I'd climbed most of the Munros, just two more summits remained, which I would tackle together, and I'd saved the biggest mountain of them all for last.

Togged out in kilts, ten of us met at Torlundy near Fort William and set out along the track signposted 'North Face'. Our route swung us left and right and on and up before we reached a stile where great views of verdant green landscape with long grasses, heathers and pines opened up. Ben Nevis's rocky north face glinted like steel in the sun, and white cauliflower clouds hatched and flourished amid the darkness of the crags, billowing upwards into a cerulean sky. Because the traverse of the Carn Mor Dearg Arete was too dangerous for my sons in winter conditions I had put off doing my final Munro outing till now, a year after our return from Nepal. I really wanted both my boys with me, but at the last minute Leon had not felt up to coming. I missed his company, but smiled as I watched Paul and Marcus ahead of me, their dark-green kilts swinging freely with each step and my friend Mel forging the way ahead of everyone else.

On the red summit rocks of Carn Mor Dearg the atmospheric conditions were dramatic. Light and dark shades were cast over the gullies, cliffs and buttresses of the Ben, and the arm of the arête, extending in a graceful, rusty curve, appeared razor sharp. The traverse was utterly involving. Rocks were slippery when it began to rain, and we became human aeroplanes, arms outstretched, until fear of falling to our doom finally forced us down onto all fours. A poor soul had died on a particularly narrow section of angled rock only two weeks earlier. After a short scramble a wide shoulder was reached before a bouldery ascent put us onto the flat summit plateau of Ben Nevis. We had ascended the mountain without meeting anyone, but here we were greeted by the sight of many people: Arabs, French, Indians and a group of Muslims sitting cross-legged in a circle, their voices praising Allah in song. It was a harmonious scene. Enveloped in white mists, our group clambered to the top of the summit cairn. Going higher still, standing on its trig point, I waved our saltire with pride, but the achievement I felt wasn't just because I'd completed the full round of Munros.

The journeys I had made by climbing all of the Munros, the trips that forced me to push the boundaries of endurance on Africa's highest mountain and on the peaks and passes of the Himalayas, had all helped me to reconcile an inner journey. Cradled in the arms of valley walls, scrambling on crags and topping out onto ridges gave me the breathing space I needed to gain perspective; in those places I was freed of troubles from the past and worries for the future. Mountains taught me to live in the here and now. They showed me that although life is uncertain, it is also full of possibility. They had enabled me to cope with my problems; but there are other ways for other people.

Nowadays I always check the weather forecast. I make sure I have my map and compass at the ready. I pack my rucksack with emergencies in mind. For as long as I am fit and able I will always return to my mountains.

Postscript

On a Sunday morning near the end of January 2017 I silenced the offending sound of my alarm and rolled over, lowering my legs over the side of the bed. I momentarily held the weight of my head in my hands; it was five-thirty in the morning. I was feeling drugged with sleep and an uncertain nagging that things were not quite right quietly tugged away inside.

Mel and I hadn't seen each other for a proper catch-up in ages, but the two-and-a-half-hour car journey to Bridge of Orchy in the west Highlands was quiet. I'd never felt such chronic motion sickness. If only my car hadn't been out of action I'd have driven and spared us both from my whimpers and moans as we curved the seemingly interminable bends on the Fort William road.

As soon as the fresh mountain air filled my lungs I felt better. And as we got moving on the long, stony track to Beinn Mhanach the heavy tiredness I'd been feeling wore off too.

We ambled up the mountainside over clumps of waterlogged grasses, and for the majority of the day we were surrounded by thick mist. The weather didn't matter. Our day wasn't about the views; it was about exercising the body and mind, and having a good old chinwag.

'There's something I'm worried about,' I told Mel. 'I found a lump in my breast.'

She looked at me. 'When did you find it? Have you been to the doctor? You've had lumps before so this one will probably be okay too,' she said. I sensed the concern through her feigned confidence.

'Yeah, I once went to the doctor with one lump and came out with several more,' I said with a laugh. But inside I felt sick. Sick because our exchange exactly echoed the very conversation my mother had had with me so many years ago.

'But it does feel different this time. It's totally solid,' I said.

Mel and I tramped on up to the exposed top. The wind baling over the summit was biting cold and, at once, the immediacy of several basic needs (warmth, food and a pee) became foremost in my mind. The mention of the lump in my breast was not spoken about again for the rest of the day.

Three weeks later I was walking with Paul, back towards his parked car, my hand in his. Dead air hung between us as we drove away from the hospital. My head was swimming. The consultant confirmed I had cancer, and it was aggressive – just like Mum's was. Sharp pain in my right breast caused me to wince. A doctor had inserted a marker – a coiled wire – into the tissue behind my nipple, so that if the chemotherapy they were going to give me shrank the tumour to an undetectably small size they would still know where to cut during surgery. Only after the operation, which I was told wouldn't be until July, would they then be able to tell if the cancer had spread to my lymph nodes. And after surgery would be four weeks of radiotherapy . . . in other words, it was going to be a tough year.

Even now every little ache or cough sends my mind into a frenzy and I think, has it gone to my bones . . . is it in my lungs . . . am I riddled like Mum was? It's hard not to feel afraid when terrible memories of what happened to her are still so vivid. She was young, fit and healthy, just like me. Her lump was small and was operated on straight away, but it had still spread to her lymph nodes. My lump was colossal in size, so did that mean the odds were that rogue cells had already split off and circulated their malicious disease elsewhere?

Am I a goner?

Is this the beginning of my end?

In the first week of 'knowing', my mind took me on a journey to hell and back several times a day. It was exhausting, and waiting to start treatment a strain. I'd had all kinds of fears about chemotherapy, but didn't give in to these – I've witnessed enough in my life to know that when the mind gives up the body soon follows. Determination to survive kicked in.

During the chemo, even when I was most unwell, I forced myself outside every day to feel the sea air on my cheeks, grateful to live right next to the beach in my beloved Ardersier. I walked. At first my body behaved like my dodgy car: motoring along at speed when suddenly, without warning, power was lost, as if I was driving with the brakes on. There was nothing I could do except adjust to the new rhythm and keep going.

But it was going to high places that I knew would restore me best, so on my good days that's what I did, I hillwalked. During the eighteen weeks of chemotherapy my feet carried me back over Meall a Bhuachaille, where I'd had that first snowy, solo walk;

to Meall Fuar-mhonaidh, my Christmas pudding hill. I tackled Munros; Bynack More and Ben Lomond. I trod new ground over a few Corbetts in Sutherland and kissed off the whole stinking chemo thing by walking the 72-mile length of the Great Glen Way, tent and pack on my back.

At first, the timing of my cancer had seemed unfair, and the irony of it was priceless – discovering the lump at age forty-four years and eighty-one days old, just one day older than Mum was when she died. But climbing made me strong. And having cancer has made me appreciate every single day of my life even more. I don't care if it's raining or windy or if the sky is clouded over. I put one foot in front of the other and off I go.

It's just another mountain.

Acknowledgements

Y ou wouldn't be holding this book in your hands if it wasn't for the following people. First off I need to thank my mate Mel, not only for her friendship, but for having a celebration birthday dinner for her fortieth. If it hadn't been for that I'd never have met her colleague and pal Fiona MacBain. Fiona, at the time, was writing her first novel. We hit it off and agreed to help each other by editing our respective stories. Fiona, in 2015, then pointed me in the direction of Pete Urpeth at Xpo North, who in turn put me in touch with the renowned literary agent Jenny Brown. Jenny read my story and said she wanted to help. I felt blown away that someone with such credibility believed in me, and cared. I don't have a degree in English or a background in writing in any professional way – in fact at school I scraped through my Higher with a 'C' pass. So, although exciting, it was a daunting prospect to face the challenge of reworking my entire manuscript to bring it up to submission standard, however throughout this process Jenny was a source of great encouragement. My editor Simon Spanton was only a WhatsApp away. Pippa Crane, and my talented publisher Jennie Condell at Elliott & Thompson both put an astonishing amount of thought and effort into all the important final decisions about how to make my story the best it could be. Thanks also to copy-editor Linden Lawson. So to all of you who have been so instrumental in getting my story out there, massive thanks.

Thank you to Hazel Macpherson, my mum's oldest friend. And to Tony Kayley for reminding me about dodgy eggs and pink radioactive sausages.

I am indebted to those of you who helped me get to the root of so many questions and for your kindnesses. Many thanks to Henry and Sara Day, and to the wonderful John and Sheila Peacock for taking me under their wing; to Laurence Smith, Jon Fleming, Neil Winship, Nigel Gifford, Crispin Agnew, Brummie Stokes, Dougie Keelan, Dr David Jones, Cattie Anderson, Sue O'Hara, Tom Lynch, John Muston and John and Durga Patchett, who all knew Gerry as a friend or colleague and were able to share their stories with me. And to Jill and Rod Owens, Gerry's cousins, thank you so much for filling in the family history. Since publication of the hardback edition of *Just Another Mountain*, Nigel Gifford has said that his recollection of the search for Gerry and his climbing partner Richard Summerton differs considerably from the account given in this book. However, the account described here was drawn from several sources including a contemporary telegram sent within days of the search taking place. But, whatever happened that day, it still brings me comfort to know that I was able to finally reunite my mum with Gerry on that mountain.

Sir Chris Bonington's generous Foreword is acknowledged with particular gratitude.

Thanks to my uncle Jimmy, uncle David, aunty Penny and Frank. Lastly, and most importantly, thank you to my long-suffering boyfriend Paul. And to my gorgeous Marcus and Leon, who are my whole entire world and without whom I am nothing. Thank you for a love which is reliable and true, and the best love of all.

Index

ABOUT THE AUTHOR

SARAH JANE DOUGLAS is a writer and artist who lives with her sons in a small former fishing village in the Highlands of Scotland. She is a lover of mountains and is proud to be Munroist number 5764. Sarah writes the popular blog 'Smashing Cancer in the Face' and actively fundraises for cancer charities.